T0370149

Selected Praise for Jesse Ball

The Divers' Game

"Jesse Ball is a writer of formal mysteriousness and neon moral clarity . . . His language is spare, strange, and evocative . . . His themes are human savagery, often state-sanctioned, and human kindness, a thin thread of resistance." —*The New Yorker*

"Jesse Ball levels a steely gaze at the very concept of humanity in this three-part novel that introduces the lower-class 'quads' and the rich 'pats,' who treat those below them with impunity. When a group of pats conceals the grisly fate of a young quad girl behind an elaborate festival, you may start to wonder just how different this dystopian world is from our own."   —*The Washington Post*

Census

"Ball's most personal and best to date . . . A point— about the beautiful varieties of perception, of experience—made without sentimentality, burns at the core of the book, and of much of Ball's work, which rails against the tedium of consensus, the cruelty of conformity." —*The New York Times*

"*Census* is a vital testament to selfless love; a psalm to commonplace miracles; and a mysterious evolving metaphor. So kind, it aches."

—David Mitchell, author of *Cloud Atlas*

"If there's a refrain running through Ball's large body of work, it's that compassion, kindness and empathy trump rules and authority of any kind . . . This damning but achingly tender novel holds open a space for human redemption, never mind that we have built our systems against it."

—*Los Angeles Times*

How to Set a Fire and Why

"The most remarkable achievement of this novel is its narrative voice . . . Sometimes, you hear the ghost of Kazuo Ishiguro's flat, chilly style. At other times . . . Borges-like parable cross-pollinates with Margaret Atwood–style dystopia."

—*The Boston Globe*

"*How to Set a Fire and Why* is a rare and startling work. Days after I read it, I find that I can't stop thinking about it, and what I've realized is that this is a book I will not forget. This is a harrowing, subtle, and absolutely electrifying novel."

—Emily St. John Mandel, bestselling author of *Station Eleven*

Silence Once Begun

"Absorbing, finely wrought . . . A piercing tragedy . . . that combines subtlety and simplicity in such a way that it causes a reader to go carefully, not wanting to miss a word."   —Helen Oyeyemi, *The New York Times Book Review*

"Ball enriches his metafictional restlessness with [a] humane curiosity . . . The language seems aware of the charged space around it, as if one were praying aloud in a darkened, empty church. His characters speak at once lucidly and uncannily; words have become strangely heavy."

—James Wood, *The New Yorker*

"Beginning as a work of seeming reportage, *Silence Once Begun* transforms into a graceful and multi-faceted fable on the nature of truth and identity."

—Sam Sacks, *The Wall Street Journal*

autoportrait

AUTOPORTRAIT
Jesse Ball

Catapult

New York

ISBN: 978-1-64622-138-7

Jacket design by Nicole Caputo
Back jacket illustration by Jesse Ball
Book design by Wah-Ming Chang

Library of Congress Control Number: 2021947245

Catapult
New York, NY
books.catapult.co

Printed in the United States of America
1 3 5 7 9 10 8 6 4 2

For Catherine Lacey

I read Édouard Levé's *Autoportrait* and found I admire its approach to biography. It is an approach that does not raise one fact above another, but lets the facts stand together in a fruitless clump, like a life. He wrote it in his thirty-ninth year. In my thirty-ninth year, this book follows his.

autoportrait

To my knowledge, I have never ridden a horse. I have ridden an elephant and a camel—when I was a child. I have ridden a human being. I have been carried while asleep and rolled on a gurney. When I was four or three I cracked my head open on a pillar. Meanwhile my brother rode his tricycle down a hill, forcing my mother to choose between us. She chose my brother. When I was six, I cut my arm in half on a glass window. The cut was lengthwise and my arm fell open like the bottom had been knocked out of a bucket. I was in the middle of a birthday party, my own, when it happened. It was comically my fault. All the other children cried at once like a chorus. Next to the place where that happened, a neighborhood boy once hit me in the face with a wiffle ball bat. He never apologized or explained why he did it and I was neither angry nor required an explanation. Perhaps we intuitively saw—things don't have explanations. I find watering plants to be onerous, and gardens even more so, but worse than that I find raking leaves, grass, or soil. I like yards to be overgrown. On the other hand I like to keep my living space in careful order, although I don't mind if it is dirty. I myself am often dirty and do not like to wash. As a boy, I would pretend to take showers by turning the water on and lightly splashing my arms. I love to take baths, however, and will do so many days in a row, if it is possible. I am frustrated by the smallness of tubs, despite the fact that I am not particularly tall. For a long time I believed I was six feet tall. I am between five foot eleven and six feet tall, but am certainly not six feet tall. When I was a boy, one of my legs was two inches longer than the other. One month everything was fine. Shortly thereafter, I had to have surgery. The options were the following: make one leg shorter by stopping its growth, or make one leg longer by breaking it in several places. I chose to be shorter, but I have often thought about how my life would have been different, particularly when reading those statistical analyses of wage disparity relative to height. I like to swim, but not for exercise. I don't like to do anything for exercise. I ran away from home a couple times, but never got far. I hate the sun and try to stay out of it at all times. This led me to lead much of my adulthood in the nighttime, though of course, I must naturally be out and about during the day, whether I like it or not. I am a parasomniac—sleepwalking. I used to sleep-talk, but stopped one day. I have night terrors and have had them since around 1990 when my brother went to the hospital and was there made quadriplegic. I have migraines, sometimes once or twice in a week, sometimes not for a month. When I do, I vomit and roll on the floor like a dog. I have had many concussions. When I was eight I was in the street and a car struck me. My mother was watching. She told the driver, you hit my boy. While saying this she realized the woman was a slight acquaintance of hers. My body was thrown some feet through the air. The reason I was in the road was—we were walking into town to buy a mechanical bird, a kind of flapping glider that could be wound up. When later I obtained it, the mechanical bird gave me no pleasure. I was left back in kindergarten and put into special education because I cannot concentrate. There are psychological documents based upon medical examinations showing that my intense hyperactivity was related to brain damage. As an adult, my specialty is concentrating, but I still cannot choose what to concentrate on. I am always ready to run and hide in the woods, if it is necessary. In such a situation, I will never be the person who is taken unawares. I did not sleep with a woman until I was twenty-two, and I believe that I confused many women in the years prior. They must have thought I wasn't interested in them. In fact, I was completely timid, but only in this regard. In all other cases, I was confident, even aggressive. The girl I slept with tricked me into her room by telling me we were going to play video games. When we got there she told me that there were no video games. She was half Mexican and a tree had recently fallen on her car. I have tried every drug I could get my hands on, but not in a social way. I was just curious about ways I could feel. Two I found best: injecting heroin, smoking DMT. I do not have an addictive personality. The phrase *addictive personality* disgusts me, and yet now I've used it. When I decide to stop doing something, smoking cigarettes, for instance, or shooting heroin, I simply stop, and there are no repercussions. One of my specialties as a young man was doing many drugs at once, too many, for instance: ketamine, psilocybin, ecstasy, heroin, cocaine, mescaline, and lots of whiskey. Somehow I never died. When I was a child, I would imitate people as a game. I would imitate my father or my mother. I would imitate my brother, too. He hated this desperately. He would try to avoid it or get away, but I would be after him, just copying copying copying. He would shout at the top of his lungs for me to stop and sometimes even then I wouldn't.

This copying of mine was not parody, though. When I copy things I try to do the best I can. I dislike cynicism, parody, sarcasm, humor that is at anyone's expense. I adore humor that picks at universal flaws, like, for instance, the fact that we have to crouch to shit, and if we don't, the shit runs down our legs. Once, as an adult I had an accident and shat while wearing my clothing. I really believed I was about to fart, but that wasn't it. If I am sleeping and someone calls on the phone, I will lie to hide the fact that I was resting. I expect everyone does this. My friend confessed to me once that he does. I didn't tell him I also do. I don't find it necessary in life to tell people what I really think. Because of that, I have an incredible variety of friends, many of whom would not like one another if they met. I am not interested in being anyone in particular, nor am I interested in having people know I am right. On the other hand, I am very competitive when playing games, and try as hard as I can to win, really to a fault. I am a good loser, though, and if I find someone who is much better than me at something, I will lose happily for years, provided that I am improving. I feel all the time that I am in their debt. I sleep for seven hours and that's fine. Sometimes I sleep for six hours and that's fine. I stayed awake in 1997 for one hundred and twenty-nine hours without stimulants. My short-term memory started to fail. If I sleep for eleven hours I become dehydrated and wake with a migraine. Since I was twenty, one of my specialties has been lucid dreaming. I am continually astonished to discover it is a subject no one cares about. I try to explain—the adventures you can have! They don't care. I love to try different sleep methods. Right now I sleep five or six hours at night and an hour in the middle of the day. The middle of the day is my enemy. If I kill myself, it will be then. I do not become melancholy at night. For years I ate everything, even insects, rotting fish, horse, but now I am a vegetarian. I love to cook and when I do I am meticulous. Unfortunately, I don't like to cook for people who aren't grateful. I am certain this is something ugly. I knew the moves of the game chess, as a boy, but didn't learn to play until I was eighteen. The smartest boy at my school taught me. His father, who once had been a correspondence chess champion, taught him. That man died and my father died and the two sons were left to play chess together. If given the choice I will often sit on the floor. I like to be at the back of anything—buses, movie theaters, et cetera. I don't like to be visible. Or I like to be the least visible I can be. I don't like chairs that suck you in, or sofas that are too close to the ground. I hate carrying on conversations while seated in such contrivances. Usually in such cases you are also forced to juggle a drink and awkwardly reach for canapés. When I enter a person's home, I look for their books, and I use these books to judge their mind. My hunches about people are often correct, in fact, uncannily so. This means it is especially bad when I am wrong. I don't like to talk about books, but I like for my eyes to be full of them. My favorite accessory a person can come bearing is a book. Of course it should be the right book. I have met a few people in my life who really loved books and I felt drastically humbled by them. One of these people treated books terribly. Most books he touched he destroyed. His house was full of piles, actual piles, of books, many with their covers half torn off and their pages ripped and bedraggled. He had read them all. He treated himself the same way. When I was young, I stole books constantly. I stole other things too, and not just in the United States, but even when I was abroad. I have never been afraid of what would happen if I went to prison. Somehow the fact that I was constantly humiliated as a child gave me a good sense of what I looked like and what it was to look at me. I have gotten away with nearly every bad thing I have done. I am not fond of smart people or dull people. I like people who are generous and who do not try to make small things sound big, people who take on their own shoulders their meaning-making. I am very happy when on public transportation, especially city buses. I am not too good for them, they are not too good for me. It is just right: a good fit. I can have very clear thoughts there. I hate being in cars unless the situation is dangerous. I like to bicycle to get places. I am a wild cyclist sometimes, and it is a cause for concern. I dislike recreational cyclists. They proceed at high speed in fancy gear and run everyone else off the road. When they are injured they never stop for one another. Instead, regular people ministrate to them. I find they have no shame. When I was in college and began to drink in earnest, I was horrified by the deformation of character it provoked in supposedly fascinating and proud people. I wondered why I would bother trying to get anyone's good opinion if all it took was a few drinks to earn someone's confidence. Worse, though, are the calculated people who will never let themselves drink a drop for fear they will be seen through. My family couldn't buy me clothes that were equal to the clothes of the children in my town. Things like this led to me being despised. As an adult, I wear the same clothes all the time, very cheap clothes. It feels good to me to not be putting myself above anyone with my dress. On occasions when I have worn a suit, I am distressed by the transformation of the world. Everyone treats you better. The thought makes me physically ill. I have no faith in people, but among people there are some real sweethearts, and that is enough, who knows how they got that way. I have met more wondrous people than I deserve. I cry easily, though for many years, I cried not at all. I love to empathize deeply with perspectives I can't understand. Of course, I fail in that. I don't believe anyone really is who they are, or at least not for long. I am greedy, but I try not to be. I eat with astonishing speed and efficiency. It disgusts people. I am done and they have taken three bites. The room disappears and there is just the plate before me, floating in a vacuum. I have received complaints about this from people who are frank. Others say nothing. Two people I've known ate at a similar or faster speed. As for me, I do everything as fast as I can. I read fast and remember very little. I walk fast and notice almost nothing. I don't know if I have ever managed to be good at something that I was not immediately good at. I have no musical talent. I carried a guitar from residence to residence for twenty-five years but never became good enough to play for anyone who I was not fucking. I tried violin, ukulele, tub bass, harmonica. Finally, I settled on an instrument that you play only for yourself—a Japanese flute. When

I try to play, my dog howls until I stop. I have been married twice. I have had a stepdaughter. I never, to my knowledge, impregnated anyone, though once I was accused of it by someone who took it back the very next day. I can vomit on command. Somehow I control this mechanism with my diaphragm. My father also could do it. I used to say I had two stomachs for this reason. When I was a boy, I learned how to masturbate in such a way that the semen does not come out. The orgasm lasts three times as long or more. I asked my doctor about it and he didn't understand. I tried again. He didn't understand. Finally, years later, I found information about it in a book on tantra. My penis is slightly bent and I found this very shameful until I realized women don't care at all. I am a competent dog trainer. I am harsh, but consistent. I believe my entire comportment is a communication with the animal in question. Similarly I try to give my dog my entire attention and learn from him about how to behave. He is one of my teachers. I don't believe dogs are bad. I believe most people aren't capable of having dogs or children. I personally would rather that they didn't. Sometimes I have trouble putting socks on, much more than usual. I never have time to figure out why. I love open windows. I like leaning out of them. I used to go out of windows onto roofs at every opportunity. I thought of windows as doors for enterprising people and I wanted to be that way. Once in high school, I got up in the middle of class and leapt out the window. For this I was disciplined. I was also suspended for fighting, for arguing with teachers, for fighting, for cutting school, and for gluing the classroom doors shut. Despite this, my high school elected me to its hall of fame many years ago in a ceremony I refused to attend. Once, in middle school, several boys were hitting me and making fun of the way I dealt with being hit. An older boy was there, wearing a cast. I dreaded what he would do, but he came to my aid. He was large and very unruly. The year before, he had set fire to the upstairs bathroom at the middle school. I was so grateful, looking into his face, I thought my heart would burst. The next year he killed himself. When I was a child, I was afraid of various things—snakes, the dark, the depths of the cosmos. After my first wife went away, I reached a place where I was afraid of nothing at all. Another way of saying that is: my fate was suddenly without interest for me. In the past, I have been effective at getting revenge on people. This is because I would do one of two things: either I would think of something clever and foolproof, and I would execute that immediately, or I would fail to do that, in which case, I would think of something simple, and I would wait awhile. At that point, the person would never guess it was me. It has been a long time since I got revenge on anyone, though, at least fifteen years. Does that mean I am less engaged in my life? I am embarrassed that I don't know enough bird names, plant names, insect names. I know plenty of animal names, car names. I love to walk and can walk very far. I have walked thirty-five miles in one day. I do not like to take pictures, though at one time I was briefly a photographer. I do not like pictures of myself, though I have noticed that in my life there were a few people who could take very generous pictures of me. The person I saw there was someone I knew.

This is not always the case. I do not like my voice, but I do like to read out loud. I don't like to read to audiences, though I have often done it. I don't like it because they are not there to hear you read. They have other reasons for being there, and cannot enter fully into the joy of being read to. Children on the other hand are pleasant to read to, the younger, the better, to a point. The most interesting people I have ever met, well, there are probably four or five of them. One was an eight-year-old girl. One was a middling old man. One was an old woman. I haven't yet met a historically great boy. I am inordinately fond of my dog, who I treat basically as a person. I like to use jars as glasses. I am completely amazed whenever I obtain another jar (by using its contents). How can it be that they give these things away? Jars are always nicer and more shapely than glasses. There is usually not enough silverware, plates, et cetera, in my home. There are enough things for two people to eat. I don't really like having people in my home, unless it is one person at a time, and that person is someone I really like. I have never lost money at poker. I have lost money playing chess. When I used to play chess in parks I would sometimes use two-dollar bills to pay my debts, that way if I saw someone else who ended up with a two-dollar bill, I would know that person could also beat me. I have never bet money playing go, but I have played go in special go parlors in fancy hotels, in Tokyo, for instance. People were astonished that I could play properly, as though I were a pine marten wearing a bow tie. The first girl I had a crush on was named Laura Fortunhoff and she was very perfect. I thought perfect was the way to go. I didn't kiss a girl until I was eighteen. No one would go to prom with me. I was a very lowly fellow. Sometimes I think my friends should have somehow shaken me bodily and I might have figured out how to be a regular person, but they didn't do that. I was a projectionist, and I love films, and sometimes girls would visit me in the projection booth, and I thought of that as part of the job. When I first got onto film, I would go to the library and get four or five movies, and I would watch them in a row. I would never have seen enough otherwise. I like to wear clothing and lots of it. The more clothing, the better. For this reason, I love winter. I like the late fall and early spring. I like to wear heavy sweaters and I like to wear coats, hats. I also like to just go around in the winter being cold. That is pleasant. I never feel so alive as when I am cold. On the contrary, when I am hot, I suffer. I hate to sweat, and much of my life has been led attempting to avoid sweating. I don't like being introduced to people. I prefer to meet them on my own terms and in my own way, or to not meet them at all. I prefer for people to know nothing about me when I meet them. If they already know things, I feel they are compromised. I enjoy not knowing about people when meeting them. It is a delight to guess how they might be, though it is usually disappointing. I dislike babies. It is my feeling that the human race is not fundamentally important. Much of my time is spent attempting to not behave like a human. This is a largely fruitless endeavor. One of my hobbies is paying attention to human-centric bias. I see it everywhere. It is amazing to me how well people manage to find others who are similarly attractive. They do it real fast, too. Of course, similarly attractive is not an objective standard, but it is fairly objective within cultures, and using that information, people are shockingly proficient. You constantly hear people mentioning that so-and-so is out of their league, et cetera. You don't hear this about curiosity or kindness. In fact, these qualities seem to make it harder to find a partner. My forearms are lightly haired. My calves and upper legs as well. I never wear shorts, and the pants I wear are heavy and loose, so my legs have areas where there is no hair, but ought to be. I have had many surgeries. These were for various accidents that I got into, for the most part, from banging my head on that column, to cutting open my arm, having my leg shortened, and others we will get to before too long. I don't mind surgery. When I am reduced to being a person without things—for instance, when I am walking to get into a pool, or lying on a hospital pallet—I feel an increase of vividness. Now I really am here, I think to myself. I am not distributed out loosely into my phone, my id, my credit card, pocketknife, pants, shoes, house keys, et cetera. For this reason, I have sometimes thought what it would be like for me to go to prison and start anew there. Once, I wrote an opinion piece for a newspaper saying everyone should go to prison. The idea of the piece is that there shouldn't be prisons, but I'm not completely sure everyone understood that. I find it very hard to write and be understood. My students at the school where I teach, on the other hand, believe people understand them deeply, and write with great confidence in that understanding. This leads to work that cannot be understood by anyone. I sometimes carry a small field glass. It allows you to look at things you otherwise couldn't. Also, you can affix a small lens to the end and it becomes a microscope, which also allows you to look at things you couldn't. On the one hand far things, on the other small things. These are the differing depths of existence. The field glass doesn't help very much, existentially, but it does give a little pleasure. People speak too loudly for me. I wear earplugs at times, and am afraid it offends. Once I looked out the window of my Chicago home and saw a man chasing after someone. He was waving a baseball bat rather insolently and shouting. The other man when he had had too much took out a very small pistol. It made a rather puny sound and he did not kill anyone but he did manage to shoot out the windows of a truck. The other man ran, as they say, as fast as his legs could carry him. It was not a terrifying scene. I am obsessed with a few texts. One is Marcus Aurelius. One is the 1855 *Leaves of Grass*. I love to read one living poet—she is Alice Oswald. I wrote to her a few years ago, but she didn't write back. I did not expect her to. When I lived in Chicago, I lived a few blocks from where Henry Darger lived. This is a man I am very fond of, though of course I never knew him. N. Lerner, who was his landlord and who discovered him, was an SAIC professor like me. I would like to think that I could have noticed how brilliant Darger's work was, but statistically speaking, the number of people who can see what is great when it appears in the guise of filth, well, they are few, and there is no guarantee that I am among them. In fact the opposite is likely to be true. One of my friends when I was a child used to kill cats in a kind of grotto near his house. What I felt about this then I don't know. There were so many ways to feel about it and I believe I felt them all at once. He was cruel also to me, of course, and years later, I received an apology letter from him. There is no use writing such a letter to the cats. I dislike computers and I dislike email correspondence. I used to like telephones, but I no longer do. It bothers me when people speak about acquaintances as friends. I don't think I should be bothered by that, but often it has led to unpleasant conversations in which I take some kind of indefensible moral high ground. I plan not to do that anymore. I eat chocolate every day, one hundred percent chocolate. This is usually made by French and Italian companies. I used to drink many coffees each day. At the moment I drink powdered green tea instead, although it is expensive. The chocolate is expensive, and the matcha is expensive. Other than that, I don't spend very much money. I have been set upon a number of times in my life. This is because of several habits I have, some of them bad. One was that I felt as a young man that I should go wherever I liked and then see what would happen. Also, there is something in me that rises when there is a question of whether some avenue should be pursued. If it seems dangerous, and I flinch from it, this something drives me on. Then sometimes unpleasant things have happened. Sometimes nothing has happened. I have unfortunately hit people in the face and then they have fallen down. Other times when I have hit people in the face they have not fallen down. The falling down or not falling down never seemed to me to have much to do with how hard the blow was. I think some people are simply unprepared to be hit, even as it happens. Of course, I have fallen down myself in this way, so I understand it. I am not an aggressive person, but I have a horrendous temper. There are many people I know who have never seen me angry. I love being sad, and in fact, it is a weakness of mine to allow myself to be sad for too long. Let someone who loves me try to comfort me, and I will just become sadder and sadder. It is better to rap me on the knuckles and walk away. My whole life I have been a terrible student. I can basically not be taught anything. If I learn myself, that's fine. There is something in the exchange of responsibility and living-investiture-in-the-body of the one taking up the learned thing that I appear to abdicate when I have a teacher. At any rate, I perform very badly and soon must give up. It is also possible that I seek teachers only for things I am in some sense incapable of really doing. One of my earliest obsessions was drawing, and it is something I still do, almost constantly. I am not good at drawing, and my drawings are incredibly and dubiously repetitive. Usually I draw foxes. In earlier periods I drew many monsters, but it has been foxes now for probably seventeen years. They wear robes and usually stand in such a way that all four of their limbs are visible. When I get a piece of paper, it is highly likely I will cover it in foxes, and that I will do that within minutes of receiving the paper. Those who have been in faculty meetings with me are familiar with the spectacle of sheet after sheet of fox-covered paper extruding from my person sequentially. I like the rain, but I don't like for my things to be wet. If I have a waxed or waterproofed bag, I can stay in the rain until I am soaked to the skin. Often, I will try to get on a bus, prior to being really wet, but once I am really wet, I will walk any distance, however long. I don't like towels—somehow they are repugnant to me. If it is possible to dry without a towel, I will do so. Other things I don't like: dryers, dishwashers, most cars, makeup, polo shirts, stores full of new home decorations. I thought I didn't like cowboy boots, but I was wrong. They are wonderfully comfortable. I was also wrong about olives, fish, yoga, et cetera. I do not eat fish or do yoga, but in earlier periods I have enjoyed them. I was taught yoga by a friend, and never went to a class. I hate being in classes. I don't like groups. I don't want to be a part of groups. I am very bad at understanding how it can be again and again that everyone else for the most part really enjoys getting together to do things. I dislike team sports with vehemence. On the other hand, I like to see people pushed almost to breaking under pressure. For this reason, I have often watched prizefighting. In this way I admire long-distance swimmers and runners. I think sprinters are not important. To me the Olympic

Games should be reestablished in such a way that the competitions are interesting. That is—the games should be well designed such that both men and women can win, and in winning, they could demonstrate a surprising synthesis of human qualities. I guess such a competition would be a cross between the Donner party, the Salem witch trials, the invention of penicillin, and making a sandwich. When I got to graduate school, I met my teacher, a famous poet, in his home. He looked at my poems and examined me carefully. You wrote these? he asked. I nodded. Well, then you are finished. You are a finished poet. Let's get you a book. I was twenty-four and I had already written several books of poems. This was exactly what I wanted to have happen, and I had felt like it was possible—I felt that one day such a thing might happen. Now I don't know how I could have believed such a thing was possible. As I said, though, it happened; he got one of the best publishers in the United States to publish the book and I had a contract a few months later. The vigor of his eyes in examining those poems is humbling to me, and as a teacher I often think, you must look at this work as if it is great. Though it is not great, you must constantly be expecting it to be great. Perhaps this was what Nathan Lerner said in his photography classes. I have always been happy to be young. Now that I am beginning to be old, I am happy to be old, too. When I am driving fast, it is generally in cars that are not good for driving fast. I am always surprised when I get a speeding ticket, because, for the most part, I manage to avoid them very well. The largest speeding ticket I have gotten was for 107 in a 55. The police officer did not arrest me. The smallest speeding ticket I have gotten was for 33 in a 30. It was in a gated community, and later there was a class-action lawsuit against the security company that gave out the tickets. I did not personally receive a check, however. At the moment, I have an old jeep that leaks in rainstorms. When you drive it 60 miles an hour it sounds like it is falling apart. The experience of being in a jalopy like that is very pleasant. When you get into an accident, you manage to assume an air of total indifference. Such grace is almost never to be found. I have friends from long ago who remain my friends. I have no idea what they think of me, but I know that they enjoy seeing me, partly because of who I was, and partly because I am carrying images of their childhoods that they have forgotten. We are valuable to each other. My family was to some extent obliterated at one point, and most of the people I know can have no sense of what my early life was. The influence of my father on my thought and behavior has been profound. I have written about my brother's influence on me. Nowhere have I written about my mother's influence. Perhaps this is because she is still alive. Many people want to have little to do with their mothers. Or if they do, the person they are having to do with is not their mother, but a mother, not so much a person in her own right as a sort of person, that sort of person, the one that pertains to them. On the contrary, I have always included my mother in my life. She has met all my friends, most of my lovers. They know her as a person, not just as my mother. Part of the reason for this is that she has no one but me. The other part is that she is interesting in her own right.

In many ways she is the opposite of me. When I went into the woods as a boy, I would often have aural hallucinations. It was usually my voice being called, from somewhere far away, but at great volume. Alternately, someone was speaking to me, someone I did not know. Later, in college, I wrote a poem about this experience, which has not survived. At the time I wrote the poem, I believe I felt I had some insight into my earlier experience. Now, years later, I believe that my insight was largely nonexistent. I am glad the poem is gone. I am not a person who is embarrassed about early work. I am pleased to see my early work, and in some sense, I stand by it. I do not believe it is work I did: obviously I was not alive then. But the person, me, who did the work, is like me in many ways. I was once the favorite in a restaurant in New York's Chinatown. I would go there and be treated with great respect and honor, despite the fact that I was an ignorant young man of little means. This was because I brought many people to the restaurant, and they in turn brought many people. My spreading the gospel of the Chinese restaurant was a known thing to the owners and staff. It got so I would never have to wait in line, would often be brought extra things I didn't order, et cetera, et cetera. Once, I brought my mother for her birthday and not only did the commotion of the restaurant entirely cease so she could be jointly appreciated, but they sent a waiter across the street to buy her an ice cream cake at their own expense. This gentle regard all came to a halt one day under circumstances too painful for me to relate. In any case: my order at that restaurant was generally vegetable steamed dumplings, scallion pancake, broccoli with garlic sauce. One such steamed dumpling would be plenty for me if I were about to be hanged. I might not even eat it. Probably I would behold it quietly, as if from a great distance. It would be enough to be able to eat it. The dumplings I am speaking of are fat and bulge. The skin of the dumplings is young skin, like that of a healthy animal. Although I want all of the dumplings when they are brought to the table, I must in any case choose one of them to eat first. Behind my house the land went uphill, first to a series of gardens, and then into the beginnings of a forest. At the latter point, a kind of attenuated cliff face bristled with vegetation. My brother and I were fond of making forts in this spot. At that time I was always on the watch for hollow bushes and hiding places. I felt there was nothing so important as to be availed of the maximum number of hiding places. Although I was a good climber, I did not often hide in trees. I expect it is because when you are discovered in a tree, you rarely manage to get away. Over many years now, I have traveled many continents and countries, and I can say with some certainty about myself that what I prefer to find in other places are: trees. Nothing pleases me like an old tree. When I come to a place, and it has no interesting trees, I want nothing more than to continue on to some other place where there might be better trees. I don't like to eat candy now, and haven't since I was a child, though sometimes as a young man, I ate it simply because there was nothing else to eat. When I was on a soccer team we practiced at a large field near the elementary school. There was a vending machine there, and those of us with thin arms would reach up into its machinery and detach sodas which we would then drink with great increase of happiness. One boy with curly hair attempted the same trick and got his arm stuck. I believe we left him there for the janitors to find. These days I have a friend with whom I go on a lot of walks. He and I sometimes don't talk. It is enough to just stand around where the other one is. There were places in my childhood, most especially the ravaged tracks beneath power lines, where older kids would go to ride dirt bikes. I rarely ever saw these riders, and I even felt that perhaps the tracks they had left reflected some earlier time, now gone. But the majesty and devastation of those places was the occasion for a great deal of wonder that stays with me even now. I am always surprised when someone remembers something I have said or done. I almost feel ambushed. Generally, I have trouble recognizing my own previous speech. At times, I disagree with whatever it was I said. On the other hand, it is a really extravagant and generous compliment when someone tells you about useful advice you gave them long ago. I very much don't like to be given books, if the book is one I don't want. In general I dislike being given presents, as I mostly don't know what to do with them. Often I immediately begin thinking about who I can pass the present on to. Something I received, when I was around eighteen, was the news that my heart does not work properly. The valves that move the blood around— at least one of them—lets the blood sluice back through it. The cardiologist told me that without medical intervention, there was a good chance I would die by thirty. In retrospect, this is an insane thing for him to have told me. The condition that I have, however unfortunate, is not cause for hopelessness. I think it was probably motivated by my father's heart death, which occurred that same year. Perhaps he was trying to put the fear of God into me, et cetera, et cetera. What he did, without perhaps intending it, was to make my behavior wild and irrational. For the next decade, I rarely took my physical well-being into account while making any decision whatsoever. As I am thirty-nine sitting here in this room writing this, you can imagine that I lasted longer than the doctor supposed. In any case, I do not blame him for his peculiar statement. Doctors must be tempted to say all kinds of things. We are lucky in most cases that they do not play jokes on us. I like very much to get into cabs, although I don't particularly like being in cabs. I very much dislike arriving anywhere in a cab. The moment when a group chooses to take a cab—that I dislike too. Of all these things, what I like least is when a group elects to take two cabs and you are stuck in a cab with one member of the group who invariably will share something, will speak to you in a way you don't want. My friends, though, are very gentle people, on the whole. They are generous to a fault. There is a kind of competition whenever it comes time to pay the bill at the restaurant. I find them all over the place. It is pretty clear from the get-go that we will be close, but sometimes it takes years for a second meeting to occur. Right now my favorite place in the world is a table by the window in a shitty diner on Western Avenue in Chicago. On this lump of red flesh, someone famously said, the face of a person without rank comes in and out. If I can get to this diner around four a.m., I am completely content. I could hear almost any news there without flinching. In fact, the last time I was there, I learned that my favorite waitress had died the day before. Although this was a shock to me, I simply let my fingers stroke the plastic of the booth and the moment washed over me. Then another moment was washing over me, and that moment said, your favorite waitress has died. Now you will order a grilled cheese sandwich and a cup of tea from a stranger and what will happen is that a grilled cheese sandwich will be brought to you, a cup of tea will be brought to you. Your waitress will be dressed in such a way that you could not recognize her and she will be laid in the ground, but there is nothing to be concerned about. How nice that you were brought grilled cheese sandwiches by her, this person who lived mostly in the nighttime. Sometimes you would smile, or she would. That's all there is to it! I have owned thousands of books, and sold nearly all of them or given them away. I have sold or given away almost everything I own. I have very little now, a knapsack, duffel bag, drawing board, pocketknife, field grass, bamboo flute, some clothing, some pots and kitchen knives. I have a few things I dislike having: a telephone, a tablet, a jeep. Some of these I can be rid of soon. I need to keep at least the phone or tablet in order to write. My last three books I wrote on the telephone. This book I am writing on the tablet. I have the jeep because I am living in Mississippi and it is not possible to go anywhere without motorized transport. There is a tree that stands outside the window of the room in which I sleep. It stands at a distance of perhaps fifty meters. I consider this tree to be my adversary. I peer at it in the darkness when I wake up before dawn. Then, when I am doing my sitting, I contend with the tree and try to make my body like a tree. In this exercise, I am without exception completely humiliated by the tree. Although I can consider the tree to be my adversary, I am not the tree's adversary. One day perhaps I can aspire to such a position. I have gone out of the house and approached the tree, and when I have done so, I can tell you it is rather different than the tree I notice from my window. One could even say they are not the same at all. Isn't it so? I have many tattoos. The first one that I got, which is most of a circle, and sits in the middle of the top of my back, was gotten with some kind of philosophical intentions. I didn't want it to mean anything, not even CIRCLE, which is why it does not properly close. That was in 2000 or 2001. Since then I have gotten all kinds of tattoos: hearts, foxes, letters, bees, wasps, bands, even the whole text of a book. People tend to assume that a tattooed person hopes the tattoo will remain perfect for the duration of the life. But the degradation of the tattoo—its blurring into a vagueness that in the final case speaks only of a profound desire, the snake writhing its way out of its skin—this is what I am looking for each time I sit for the needle. Why should I not choose to adorn this dirty skin-sack with arcane symbols and outlines of animals or plants? At a house on High Street in 1992, a boy and I would read the volumes of a role-playing world called Rifts. We never really played the game. We just made character after character for ourselves in a ceaseless act of redefinition. My characters were always as elusive as I could make them. His were staunch, fair-minded. I would try to use any loophole I could find to have the best character I could. This behavior was beneath him. Generally, he named all his characters the same name. That name was Stilgar. I have an ongoing battle about my hair with the person I love. I like to shave my head about once a month. She prefers I have ordinary hair. This leads to a situation where now and then I placate her and grow it out, and then tumultuously I return to a period of doing what I like again. As I have gotten older, I find I hate reading more and more. That is, reading what I don't want to. Reading the necessary things, my few favorites, is always the deepest pleasure, or not even a pleasure so much as the ongoing reconstruction of my moving domicile. Like a bagworm making its bag, I read in order to effect a shield. Now and then my face protrudes to bite at a leaf. There is a portrait by Andrew Wyeth of a boy sitting in some brush. He is wearing a coonskin cap and clasping his legs in his arms. He is booted and his pants appear to be denim. His look is furtive. The face moves powerfully out of the portrait toward you; it exceeds all the rest, like the faces in Klimt. The power of the face is held in check only by the monotony of the grasses, the brush. Stalks cross and lie in broken verticality, so many. In contravention of this, the face that seems to receive it. I have always felt this was a portrait of myself as a boy. Or not that. I have always felt that this portrait of a boy *is* me. Not the boy being portrayed, but the portrayal. My toes are rather straight at the end, like a ballerina's, as they say. Sometimes when I am playing a game with someone, I will give them friendly and good advice and sometimes this advice leads them awry. It is the right advice, but they are usually thinking of winning only that game, the one we are playing, whereas proper strategy is behavior that leads to the maximum number of wins over time. Explaining this proves useless. My hands are well shaped and extremely strong—much stronger relatively than any other part of me. My eyesight is good. It was better, of course, before, but I still see without a prescription. My eyes are green and brown and yellow and blue. Sometimes they are bluer, sometimes grayer or greener. I suppose it depends on the surrounding colors and light. My eyes do not serve me well, in some sense. They seem to let in too much light, because I am hurt by it, and have to wear sunglasses. I have to flinch away in movies and look at the back of the seat in front of me. I don't know really why this is, but it generally presages a coming migraine. If I turn a corner in the street or look to the side and see the sun in any fullness, it is the same: a migraine begins without fail. I have gotten very good at noticing it, but if I do not have the medicine, knowing is useless. Having migraines is both fortunate and unfortunate. It is unfortunate for obvious reasons: there are many times when one doesn't want to live anymore, especially if the migraines follow one on the next, day after day. It is fortunate because the hour of life that unfolds when a migraine has passed contains such ascendancy—I doubt anyone not a migraineur has felt it. Is there any other pain so intense that passes away completely into harmony? My friends and I used to hit one another a lot and fight or mock fight. You were always in danger of being grabbed up or smashed down or pushed over. One of my friends was twice the size of me but we would fight like alley cats. Someone picked on me in the auditorium of the middle school on High Street. That building is no longer a middle school, but in any case, my friend laughed. This so incensed me that I turned on him and attacked him. I didn't attack my insulter. I was probably too afraid. My hair is wavy and brown and thick. This meant that I could do nothing with it as a child. In fact it served as a punishment—or an incitement to the same. My mother cut it badly and it was an advertisement to others of my weakness. For a long time, I thought my bones would never break. I was in all manner of accidents, and . . . nothing. I could be lacerated, bruised, et cetera, but no bone would break. Since that time, I have broken an ankle and cracked a rib. My knee has been wrenched to bits. A bone-boss grew up in the middle of the back of my hand. My spine was compressed and it spat out some of what keeps it from clacking together. These incidents were mostly from various kinds of roughhousing, whether in martial arts or the world. None of it was really necessary, and I question my whole approach to physical preparedness. Yet I am glad to have found my balance now. I wake in the morning, I sit, I walk long distances. If there is somewhere to swim, I may swim. If I have a bicycle, I will ride it, especially to meet someone. There is no more preparing for me to do, other than preparing for death, and I do that by laughing. Not laughing at death, of course. Laughing at myself. I love to nap on the floor of the house with my dog. My whole life I could never nap because I would wake in panic. But napping with my dog seems to solve that, as does being on the floor. I prefer not to answer questions about myself, what I have been doing, et cetera. Because of that, I tend to assume others do not want to answer such questions. This leads to a failure on my part of inquisitiveness in conversation. I believe it can even be hurtful. Something else I fail to do: give compliments. I find that giving compliments is not fundamentally important, indeed, in art-making it is very harmful. Since I spend a good deal of time teaching art-making, you could imagine I don't give compliments because of that, however, I think the not-giving of compliments preceded the pedagogy. To my mind, if you love someone, you will spend time with them, and that spending of time is indicative of the love you feel, more so than anything you will say. Of course, sometimes one loves a person and simply cannot spend any time with them. Perhaps then a word or two is necessary. I read very rapidly. Often I read a whole book straight through, even if it is a long book. After reading, I rarely remember much of anything. The opposite case was my father, who read unbelievably slowly. The reason for this was, when he had read a paragraph, he would ask himself if he could reconstruct what had been written; if he could he would continue. My father remembered much of what he read and was an authority on things factual. At that time there was no widespread internet use, this was the 1980s: people would call us on the phone to ask my father questions. They were certain he would know and often he did. Once someone called and asked, What is that Italian specialty, you bake it in a casserole dish? He looked at my mother uncertainly and said into the phone, Lasagna? Yes, that's it, the person replied. Thank you. I feel uncomfortable in stores, uncomfortable buying things, uncomfortable especially trying things on. I felt extremely comfortable years ago when I would steal things. Then I knew what I was doing in the stores. I knew who I was standing there, who I was as I moved, what I should look for. But when there as a person who will buy things, no. I am in dismay. My father was completely addicted to book-buying. Although we had little money, what money we had was mostly spent on books. He did not live very long and I do not think it possible that he could have read all the books he bought. I know in my own case, I have read only some of the many books I have owned. In fact, I encourage my students to constantly discard books that they find unsuitable. It is advice I take. Some of my friends read. Some do not. Many are afraid to tell me so, as though, because I am a writer, I am a total advocate for reading. Listen, people can do what they want, that's what I would say if asked, but the people I meet who pretend to read just go on pretending. I imagine it is hard to read if you read only a handful of books per year. It is a habit, a kind of vocation, to submerge yourself in book after book. Once it is what you do it is neither easy nor hard, but at the beginning, I think it is hard. In my own case, I love theater, but I almost never go because it is so unutterably bad. The same is true of film: I adore great film, but the films that people make are tedious and nonsensical. For cinema it is wonderful to live in a great metropolis because there will be showings of films that are worth seeing, and then, of course, one wants to watch in a crowd. As for literary readings, I go only when dragged. My opinion is that they have nothing to do with books. It is an interesting thing about a good book that almost nothing is ever substantively said about it, nothing written, nothing said, that is worth attending to. The best speech about books is just the injunction: read this one. If the person who speaks it is remarkable, perhaps the book will be so. I love hot dog stands. Nowadays I don't go to them. I like to travel by train. This is especially true on those lovely European fast trains. I have, however, traveled by train in other places, like Japan and China. The Japanese trains are like the European trains, or even superior in some cases. The Chinese trains are like nothing I previously knew. There is a hard sleeper and a soft sleeper. I believe we chose the hard sleeper. My friend slept on a bunk behind me, and I sat on the bunk, surrounded by curious people, people sitting on other bunks, sitting on my bunk, people sitting on the floor. We talked all through the night and shared provisions of various kinds, many of which I did not recognize. People would come and go. It was a shifting crowd—and everyone eager to give and to have. For a while, I would meet a man who was a Chicago policeman. We would go to the police station in Chicago and there was a judo room. There we would battle and I would always lose. He was very good, smaller than me, but really profoundly strong. Jiujitsu was a specialty of his. I am very bad at it, but I am game and don't like to give up. He taught me a little of something that is, wonderfully, called spider guard. I am a sucker for things that are named well. I once tried to learn an entire defense in chess just because it is called the

Hedgehog. When I was younger I used to go in for feats. Somehow I thought it was important for a person to do them. The advice I most often give my students is to contradict themselves. Please, I say, please please please contradict yourself. Who do you think you are? I like to live in different places, but when I do, I invariably end up doing the same thing. I think this is a good reason for wanting to move around. What I do is: sit, walk, read, draw, go to cafés, cook. I like to drink whiskey. I like to drink some beer, but not most beer. I like to go to fancy bars and also lowdown places. When I go anywhere, I like to sit at counters. The place in the world where I feel the calmest is a bathroom, especially one with an open window on a second or third story, especially if no one is coming and there is no reason I should be there. The greatest relief of my life was fleeing school. I would flee the class-room and go to the various bathrooms and always I had a favorite. Or I would flee entirely, out of the building and into the woods, or the town, or the cemetery. That feeling of escape is the best I have ever known. I like to fill out forms: for instance, entry forms on airplanes. I like to do this only if I can do it with a pen. I like to write very small. In a way, I feel that my writing very small on the form is some sort of defeat of the form. I have always liked taking tests in this way—not to defeat the other people who are taking the test, but to defeat the test itself. One thing that is generally unfair about tests is that before they test anything else they first test reading speed. In my estimation, oral examination is superior to every other form of examination, but it is rarely ever used in the United States. When I go to a person's studio to look at the work they have been doing, I wander in aimlessly, as if I am confused. I mope about, glancing here and there, not looking at anything in particular. I am trying to feel what the person is after, what is their central concern. Usually the artist has been told that x or y is the thing they do, but in truth it is something else. I then ask lots of questions, very simple questions. After a while I excuse myself. My first girlfriend in college was a painter and I remember how powerful I found it that she would extract these paintings, it seemed to me, from the inside of her body. There was one in particular that I loved, a giant lying on the floor of a room, and on top of him there was lying someone else, someone of ordinary size. The magnificence of a person striving with the world, striving to speak at all, whether with a brush or a pen or a gesture, I felt it so thoroughly in her ambition, when I would visit her there in her studio. This is something I think about now when I see the work of these young people, now, when I am no longer awed by the spectacle of making. Then I have to squint my eyes to see it again. I have a replica Roman game piece made from resin that I bought long ago in France. To me it stands at the heart of my life and existence. I don't know for what game it was intended, but the game piece is round and in relief there is a sculpture of a rather foolish-looking man riding on a rooster. As soon as I saw this, I knew that this was me through and through. I never felt so understood. I used to carry it around with me, but now I know that is not necessary. Once I lost a game of handball for fifty dollars. At least a hundred people were watching. My anger is very large. When I am angry, I think very clearly and make verbal assassinations of every kind. I do not lie or invent things in order to win, but I do say things that should never be said, simple, plain, awful things. My anger, like all anger, is never about the thing in question. I am almost never angry these days. Perhaps I have been angry once or twice in the last years. I feel it is a statement about me, a failure on my part, an inaccuracy I try to avoid. That I should be so low to be angry. There is a sort of person, however, who tries to establish the limits of their behavior by testing and testing until they have found the frontier of your anger. Then they turn back. What can one do with such a person? I try never to be angry, as I said, but I do not try to not be sad. For me, being sad is a kind of occupation. I love the mellow sadness that is simply feeling everything that has been lost, everything gone. I like, too, the horrible encroaching grief of feeling what will be lost, that what stands whole before you will be impossibly and hideously rent and ruined. When the screw twists in the belly and this thing is really felt! To let these feelings come and to let them go again like guests. I feel about writing and about art that one's gift is the size that one permits. If a person believes that the work is grudgingly done, is tortured, that every iota must be tallied and kept, then it will be so. Likewise, if one feels that the work appears like the absence of fog, and goes away again with a gentle dimming, appears, goes away, appears, goes away, that one has little do with it and one can simply give the things one makes, handing them off to others endlessly until there is no volition or energy in the limbs—if one feels that way, then that will be so. And how much better to have it be that way, an endless gift of which you have no ownership, for which you deserve no credit. I like to see people boiling pasta. I find it exciting. The more pasta, the better. If I see some footage of one of those Japanese kitchens where people are lifting enormous quantities of noodles in sieves I am almost beside myself. I am good at throwing things, and can throw them farther and more accurately than most people I know. Once there was a snowball fight I was involved in as an adult and I hit a girl in the face with a snowball. I think I did it on purpose. I thought she was pretty. One of my shoulders stands higher than the other. My left hand is quicker than my right, but weaker. When I played soccer for my high school, I scored goals with both feet. Once I scored a goal on a corner kick. The goalie caught the ball, but landed inside the goal. I was named the athlete of the week for my high school. People thought this was funny because I was such a loser. I like the notes that irascible old writers write about wanting to be left alone. These are often typed on typewriters and that pleases my eye. I also like sets of rules that were posted in workplaces in the past, newsrooms, gambling dens, et cetera. When I worked as a croupier on a reservation in New Mexico, there was an old man who would strike me under the table with a cane if he didn't like the cards he got. For some reason I did not report him, although it happened many times. Other croupiers I spoke to had shared my experience. Likewise, they had not reported him. A man wanted to fight me once for taking his money. I told him he would have to wait until my shift was over, five hours later. When I went out to the parking lot, he was not there. I wear the same thing every day, a janitor's outfit, blue button-down shirt and blue pants. This makes everything simple for me. Once in Iceland, I broke my ankle doing judo. Someone threw me and my ankle clacked against the floor and that was that. Even though the entire floor was on springs, it didn't help. I had to walk home with the broken ankle. By the time I got home, I could almost not get the boot off. I remember it was snowing and I kept falling down. I like to look at fire hydrants, and treat them affectionately, mostly in the abstract. I like to leave windows open, but I am concerned about insects coming into rooms. I hate fluorescent light. I dislike when restaurants put special fire gouts in their outdoor areas as a flamboyant gesture. Sometimes when I am given something delicious in a bag, I will walk a long distance before eating it, basically for no reason. I will end up sitting on someone's lawn eating a taco. This is a behavior I have noticed in my dog, who will sometimes take food from his bowl and go elsewhere with it. When I was sixteen, I enjoyed ordering egg sandwiches at maximum speed:

baconeggcheesesaltpepperketchup. They would give me two small orange juices in tiny cartons which I would throw in the garbage. A man lived on a street I would often walk down. He was probably thirty-five or forty and wore a Bronx Science letter jacket. This loyalty to an old high school confused me deeply. I do not think it is important to read a lot or to read a great variety of things. I think it is important to read something and to take it entirely into your body and find yourself changed by its company. I have read a great deal of Western philosophy and I find much of it beside the point. There are exceptions: some Pre-Socratics, David Hume, Marcus Aurelius, Meister Eckhart, Diogenes. The tradition went the wrong way with Plato, who is wrong about a horrifying number of things, and whose wrongness is perhaps exceeded only by Aristotle and those that follow him. As for the Christian philosophers, the less said, the better. When someone offers me something, I desperately want to accept it, but I have become better about not doing so. My second wife was an aerialist and sometimes we would go to the park. I would climb a tree and hang silks from it and then she would swing around on them for hours. An old woman approached us one time, and said that she was a Playboy bunny from long ago. She had been the centerfold of an issue in the early 1960s. Right then she was feeding grain to pigeons. She wanted my wife to know that her performance was very beautiful, and that probably everyone who could see it was pleased. In the years between eighteen and twenty-five, I used to hit things a lot and break them: doors, walls, et cetera. I fought a lot. I would roam around in a sort of haze. I went to graduate school and was horrified by how little the other students loved books. I would commonly catch them walking around without a book. If they had to speak about books, they would say things that didn't make sense. For them being a writer was not so much about books. Once one of my professors used the word *retard* in a lecture and got a bunch of laughs. I left the hall, saying to myself, this place has nothing to do with me. I once wrecked a motorcycle in the desert. I was on it and a girl was on it. She was mostly fine. I demolished my knee. The knee was so ugly that when we got to the hospital the doctor in the emergency room waited six hours for the next shift to come on so he wouldn't have to deal with it. When I lived in France, I noticed that old French people commonly pour water into their wine in order to make it last longer. Out of the window of the house I lived in, which was on the fourth story, you could see, at the corner of the street, a garbage can some distance away. The curvature of an object's movement through space under the influence of gravity was such that it was possible to simply push a piece of garbage gently toward the distant can and it would float down in an arc and land there. Of course, sometimes we would miss, but for the most part, not. Two workmen observed me do this from below and one gave me a toothy grin. I like to eat different things, but I also like to eat the same thing. Once I ate only chocolate chip cookies for breakfast for two years or more. I had decided to become very thin and this was part of my plan. It worked perfectly. The mother of a friend of mine grew up during the famine in Greece and she told me that it is a good thing to leave a little food on your plate. People know then that they fed you enough; also, they know you have enough to eat at home. Almost pathologically I eat everything put in front of me, although I repeat my friend's mother's words again again again. In 1999 one of my ears became entirely blocked. I could hear nothing out of it. A nurse put some kind of acid in the ear and the next day I came back and they extracted a gigantic hunk of bloody wax. The hour following this was one of the most beautiful of my life: I could hear again, almost supernaturally. I have traveled to foreign countries to promote my books, and in doing so, have noticed that people don't really like them anywhere, not here, and not in foreign countries either. There are a few people living who do. When they die, I imagine they will be replaced by a few more. There is a perfect living arrangement that I am forever looking for. It is a sort of boardinghouse situation with a pretty bare room. The trouble is, it takes place in a completely different time. I can find it nowhere that I look. I dislike the sentimental. Even less, though, do I like supposed truth-tellers whose nihilism is just the bimodal brutality of a child. In fact, both things are true: the world is horrible; it is also cause for ecstasy. My mother lied to me a few times when I was a child, once famously. My father, to my knowledge, did not lie to me. One of my most painful memories is when he brought me home a toy. It was winter in the early to mid-1980s. My family was rather poor. Certainly it was a big deal to receive a toy. My father came in the door from work and the cold came in with him. I was sitting on the far side of the kitchen table. He set down his briefcase and opened it. He didn't even take off his jacket. He handed me the package. It was Darth Vader. I looked at him and cried because I wanted Luke Skywalker, not Darth Vader. There are many ways in which this was the wrong thing to do. Again and again the scene replays in my head. I find stairs to be wonderful and stairwells likewise. I like the closets under stairs. I like the doors to roofs that sometimes stairs end in. I will climb out a window and go along a ledge to get to another place. I will crawl under something heavy, say, a vehicle, to get somewhere. I have gone over many barbed-wire fences of various descriptions, once, even, while carrying a bicycle. A friend of mine and I crossed a train trestle over the Hudson River and when we reached the far side, found an uncrossable fence stopping our progress. We crossed it by jumping off the roof of a shack that abutted the fence. I have been guilty sometimes of leading people into trouble too deep. I suppose I myself was not intending to get out of it. Yet get out of it I did. Heroin is an example of this. Isolation and hermit-like life is another. I feel better when I am around people I do not know very well. Sometimes when I am in the out-of-doors I get the feeling that the world would prefer there were no humans. I understand that this is also a sentimental view. At one time I was an eater of escargot, which is essentially equivalent to eating sticks of butter, something no one does. As a child, I was asked what I would wish for if I could wish for anything. People mentioned world peace. A boy next to me said a Ferrari. I said that I thought there should be a plague that would wipe out four fifths of the human population. The farthest I have ever run is six miles. I have climbed a few mountains, among them Mount Fuji. The highest thing I jumped off was fifty or sixty feet. The longest thing I jumped over was a creek in the Great Smoky Mountains. Someone else jumped over it, I jumped over it, and the third guy did not. He elected to walk some distance to where there was a bridge. Being stung by things doesn't bother me much. I was constantly bitten by spiders in my childhood home. Once, I woke and the ceiling was covered with them. Around that time, I was pretty sure something was going on with my room. Often there would be people in it I didn't know who would stand around the bed while I slept. The first time I ever thought about the Great Matter, the matter of life and death, was when I learned that the sun was eventually going to collapse. In that moment I felt a total certainty that almost everything I had ever been told was a lie. Furthermore, I realized that life was just being in this body. That's it. I fell into a horrible depression that in some ways has lasted until today. For some reason, I have almost never been hungover. I would hear people complaining about hangovers, but I had a hard time understanding what it was they meant. When I sleep, I like to have part of one leg out of the sheets. There is a passage in Hemingway where the old man wakes the boy by holding his foot. My father often woke me this way. I prefer hard mattresses and thin mattresses to soft mattresses. I would rather be cold than hot. I like the room I sleep in to be rather chilly, but I do not like air-conditioning. I sometimes think that not enough information about toiletry, the wiping of asses, is shared. I feel someone must have a technique that is substantially better than the usual method. I am curious about what that is. I do not like being left in bed. I prefer to be the first one up. I hate waking up to find people gone. Once, I was obsessed with a video game, so much so that I would jump out of bed in the morning just to begin playing it. The first thing I was really good at was handball, a sport that is played against walls in New York. It is a lowly sport, played by misfits and slovens, although the courts were put up all over the U.S. in the 1960s in order to promote physical fitness. I was so good at it that I would play adults and beat them for money. Sometimes I would pretend to be lefty and then switch. I would play two people at the same time. These successes were important later when I began to publish, because I knew that I did not have to alter what I was doing; rather I should wait until it was recognized for what it was. I enjoy very much seeing beavers and cormorants. Their liminality calls out to me. I read recently that beavers are going to exacerbate global warming by building dams all over the Arctic. This is the most pleasant vision of the apocalypse that I can think of. I like burrowing owls. I like donkeys. Less than that, in fact not at all, do I like pretty birds, large cats of various kinds, showy lizards. I like hyenas very much. I like rats. I am a real enjoyer of pigeons. Seeing them huddle in the minus-10 cold in Chicago is very sad. Sad also is seeing the bodies of the ones who could hold out no longer. Meanwhile I stand there wrapped in two coats. When I first kissed a girl I was eighteen and I did not know how to do it properly, but it went all right. She had the largest breasts of any girl I would subsequently end up with, and I had no idea what to do with them. Her handwriting was very good. For years I didn't like mushrooms, olives, powerful cheeses. When I was about twenty, all this changed. My grandfather loved pistachios and I thought this was a sign of his villainy. My mother identifies plants, herbs, trees, wildflowers, et cetera, with abandon. She knows things about them too, what people used to use them for. I feel this is why she can remember all that information. I used to visit a prison for about six months. Doing so made it clear to me that there is a war between the government of the United States and her own citizens, and it has been going on forever. In restaurants, I am a good tipper. I do not want my things carried for me, so I do not tip doormen or bellboys who lunge for my knapsack. In the morning when I have woken up, if I am alone in bed, I like to adjust to a position where my legs are at a right angle to the rest of me. The feel of the bed—the temperature of the new places my legs and trunk are resting—is refreshing. I feel then a slight movement in my metaphorical heart, in the gauge that judges what or how I can look forward. I have fallen out of trees. I have climbed onto moving trains, and on moving trains I have climbed onto the train's roof. I was caught doing both things, once on the LIRR and once on the New York subway. I used to jump the turnstile often. I was never caught doing that. I have never been pickpocketed, although I had to travel once very far to help a friend who was. In Kashgar, my friend and I observed a man using long silver chopsticks to pick a pocket. This was almost not to be believed. The most brilliant person we met there was a child prostitute who tried to sell himself to us. We spoke to him for a long time in the shadow of a mosque. I have never wanted to be wealthy or to live in a big house. The things I am jealous of are things people can't control, like surviving a train wreck. For a while, I thought a lot about being a person who survived a train or airplane accident, and how it would affect my career. This was a useless line of thought. I do not wash my clothes very often—probably not often enough. I hate the word *snack*. I learned Spanish very badly in school and spoke it poorly when I lived in Mallorca. I forgot most of it and learned French poorly on my own and spoke it when I lived in Pau and Montpellier. Then I forgot French when I learned Icelandic, which I spoke for some years with my Icelandic family. Although my Icelandic was perfectly reasonable I have since forgotten it. Once in the basement of the house of my guitar teacher, I handed him a tape. The tape contained the music I was hoping to learn. He put it in a stereo and listened. It was something by the blind musician O'Carolan, something very complicated, being played on a Celtic harp. This was Long Island in 1992. My guitar teacher was in a hair band. He was training to be a physical therapist, if I recall correctly. Nonetheless, he listened to this Gaelic tape and then stopped it. He retuned his guitar to a new and invented tuning. Then, without pausing, he played the Celtic harp piece for me and wrote it out in tablature. For him it was actually nothing. Rarely since then have I seen such a shocking thing take place, and with so little fanfare. I tend to go up stairs quickly and down them slowly, although if I can put my hands on opposite banisters or walls, I will go rapidly down. In the subway in New York,

I would often slide down the banisters, a thing which gave me incomparable joy. I like to piss outside and I like especially to piss on things, buildings, statues, et cetera. My dog likes to piss where I do. Thus, often I will pee on something and he will follow. I have had six cats: Fluffy, Tiger, Cools, Nora, Salazar Larus, and one more. I have had two rats: Nun, Klara. I have had three dogs: Pope, Flea, Goose. The best cat I have ever known is owned by a friend of mine. This cat is a Russian blue named Twinkie. Its behavior is that of an affectionate dog. I do not really enjoy using pencils, although I want to. I am particular about what pens I have. I don't care for ballpoint pens, fountain pens, et cetera. I like fine-point drawing pens. Robert Walser used to cut a pencil very finely and use it to execute extraordinarily small handwriting. This is what I want to do, but I have not found it in me. Some of my heroes: Ryōkan, Walser, Elizabeth Cotten, Gaston Bachelard, Walt Whitman, Marina Tsvetaeva. I believe that all monuments to war should be torn down. I do not believe WWII was a just war. I do not like to hear people praised for violence. On the other hand, all human things have some interest, and there are stories in wars that I, like everyone, am curious about. My greatest hatred is for established religions: Christianity, Islam, Judaism, Hinduism, Buddhism, et cetera. What horrible things have been done beneath these banners! I dislike when songs are stuck in my head. They are rarely songs I like. I have wondered what the mechanism is by which this occurs. I have a very bad memory and often forget things. I am especially bad at knowing people's names. I have a disrespect for names: I do not think they are important. Still, people who remember names move fluidly through rooms, clasping hands, smiling, greeted and greeting in turn. Meanwhile, I am looking at my feet. At various times I have kept journals, diaries, et cetera. These include my thoughts, drawings, diagrams, lists, and such. When I lived in New York City, I was frustrated by people looking over my shoulder on the subway, so I began to write the journals backwards. Writing backwards is an easy parlor trick anyone can do. But it is very useful. Now I do not like to keep journals, but instead tear ordinary sheets of paper into four and carry around one or two at a time. After I have written on them I generally discard them. I don't like having anything to do with my bank, because I am sure the news will be bad. But the news is rarely bad. I have fallen asleep while driving, but only for a few seconds at a time. I have been in trucks that rolled, cars that spun, and convertibles that almost flipped. On a flight in 2010, the turbulence was so bad that many people started to cry. A businessman clutched at the hand of the person next to him. On we swooped through the air. I was delirious with happiness. A very long time ago I read a quote that said, you can be rich by having lots of money or by learning to need almost nothing. I am going the second route. One of the happiest moments in my life was in my hometown at a shitty little restaurant. My friend and I were maybe ten and we had a basket of fries in front of us. There were just so many fries. I was looking at them and thinking—this fry-eating thing is not going to end anytime soon. We would take our money and buy comic books and candy but I was not allowed to have candy and my mom would sometimes appear in town and confiscate it. This led to me eating everything rapidly, a habit I retain. Anyone who has watched birds knows how cruel they are. A person with a heart can only watch for so long, especially water birds: ducks, geese, swans, gulls. They behave with the unending sadism of children—but what's worse, there is no sadism there! They just want all of whatever there is. In general, I am suspicious of handsome men. I find they are more ignorant than their less attractive peers. I dislike it when people say my name out loud. My middle name is William. I find this to be an imposition. If I had to come up with a name for myself it would be something like Bagworm. I would be comfortable responding to that. Once, leaving a bowling alley, a girl kissed me. Another time, when I was working as a kind of bartender, a girl kissed me also. These stand against the thousands of times I wanted someone to kiss me but no one would. There were some years in the nineties when I wore a baseball hat compulsively. Teachers scolded me to take it off. I have never liked sports teams. It saddens me to see how team sports robs the populace of the U.S. of their rightful anger and energy. I have argued successfully before a judge. Once, I was asked to leave a bus. In Ohio, I fell asleep on a Greyhound and woke up with someone I didn't know, an older man, asleep on my shoulder. I am impressed when people use calipers to measure things. When pets or children do things that don't make sense, I look around for a plausible explanation. The blocky shapes of sheep exult me. The strip malls in Long Island fill me with terror. I somehow believe I can be trapped there. I don't like when people do things at the same time. Therefore, I dislike ceremonies, chanting, synchronized swimming, pair-diving, maneuvers, military funerals, et cetera. An exception is, I like when a child has been lost and people comb the country in a long line. I badly injured my hand once, when I was assaulted while bicycling. This forced me to change my handwriting. My hands shake horribly all the time, and have my whole life. Possibly this was part of why the psychiatrist believed me to be brain-damaged. In any case, to have reasonable penmanship was a large work. I don't believe, as Steiner does, that handwriting gets to the heart of a person. But I don't believe there is a core to human beings. I think we are hollow vessels that boat through these waters, changing and changing amid things that change themselves. However, I spent a lot of time on my handwriting and was forced to change it after that fight. I moved the pen from between my thumb and forefinger to a new position, between my forefinger and middle finger. Previous to that, I tried to write left-handed, but the results were poor. The new position gave me the uncertain writing and drawing of a child. I was given a thousand dollars once to speak somewhere, but had to have a nice suit of clothes in which to do it. This ended up costing most of the thousand dollars, and I have since used the suit at several funerals. I thought that for public speaking it was important to be prepared. At first I would write down what it was I was going to say, perhaps I even tried to memorize it. Or if not that, then I would have the text of the speech with me on the stage. My approach now is to go onstage completely unprepared, like a zoo animal. The zebra goes onstage and what happens? There's a zebra onstage. One of the worst things I ever saw was in DC. My friend and I had been out at a jazz club and we were walking down the street. The police had collared a guy and they were trying to put him in a van. He busted loose and ran out into the street. At that moment a truck appeared right where he was. They were both trying to be in the same spot and the truck smashed him down. But his hands were behind him, in cuffs, so there was nothing to break his fall. His head slapped against the asphalt and broke open. We were perhaps fifteen feet away. When I learn that someone doesn't like to be surprised or scared it makes me want to surprise and scare them. Once upon a time, I would tickle people, my stepdaughter, for instance. I now believe people prefer not to be tickled. Once I was walking in San Francisco and found a person who seemed to be dead. I found this person by stepping over him and then stopping. A nearby police officer could not confirm the man's status. I prefer pine trees now, although as a child I was a great lover of deciduous trees. The quiet of pines pleases me, and the moribund order that exists beneath their branches. The shack that I want is on a hill and surrounded by a grove of pines. I am obsessed with the book *Hōjōki*. It is clear to me from reading books that people aren't smarter now than they were three thousand years ago. Of course, much valuable knowledge has been unearthed. But largely people don't know it. I have a friend with whom I have competitions. Some of the competitions we have had include: a foot race, sitting on a chair longest when you are not sitting on a chair, arm wrestling, grappling, fasting, body-fat percentage, pull-ups. I have lost only one of these, unfortunately it was the one that was for the highest stakes. I have never been to North Africa, sub-Saharan Africa, the Middle East. I love to cook North African food, however, and do so often. My oldest friend was a soldier in Iraq. The first book I read that treats these countries at all is one of my favorites: Herodotus. For a while, I wasted my time telling my students to read books that I love. I have had several amazing students. I think I am lucky in that. Each time it is the same: they show up and are wonderful and I watch as people (other students, teachers) come up with ways for them to stop being wonderful. Meanwhile, I tell them to ignore everything. Eventually, they leave, just as wonderful, but older. I am not using *wonderful* as a blank superlative. I mean, actually, they are full of wonder: they wonder about things, they themselves are a wonder, they produce wonders. When you ask such a person a question, you get something back that was already yours, something you had forgotten—or you get something new, something you have never encountered. In a moment it is an old friend. Really we are all like this, can all be like this. It is only our sad grasping protectiveness that makes us monsters. I am an energetic and talkative drunk, though I am rarely drunk. I become expansive. I never had a measure of my cognitive impairment while drunk until I began to play chess online. Then I would sometimes play while drinking and I would see that the rating I could demonstrate while drinking was rather lower than usual. This was disturbing, but perhaps obvious. Even more disturbing: the rating I could demonstrate usually is not in fact consistent at all. One morning, feeling great, I can play chess at one level, another morning feeling equally great, I play drastically worse. This has bearing because it would be lovely to know at what cognitive level one is operating prior to attempting particularly difficult tasks, for instance, writing a crucial part of a novel. Another perspective is: the shamanistic leap that should take place in writing, the departure of oneself from one's body into some communal shape, that is enough to allow the work to take place properly. Perhaps such a thing happens with professional chess players. When people break things of mine, I am very nice about it. I find it unpleasant to be cut in line and have spoken up about it upon occasion. There have been some garments I enjoyed owning. One was a pair of shoes that I had re-soled five times. They were black and very simple. The leather at the end was like my father's face. As a boy I had a sweatshirt, much too large for me, that I wore with an extravagant happiness. It said "B.U.M. equipment" on it. This act of self-negotiation was appropriate to me then and would be so now. The third was also a sweatshirt, which I wore as a winter coat for a number of years, made by Carhartt. Its end was its use as a coffin for my rat Nun when I buried her in the yard of a house at Schiller Street in Chicago. The coolest piece of clothing I have owned was a black raincoat made of heavy rubber. It was very ruthless-looking and would be verbally praised by extremely tough people whenever I came across them. One time in particular, I was crossing a yard behind a cafeteria and some of the workers from the cafeteria, older black men, were smoking cigarettes on the concrete steps. Two of them called me over and tried to buy the raincoat from me. I think that now I would sell it for some low amount, but then I did not realize how pleasant it is to pass on things of value rather than to keep them. I was very proud standing there in my rubber coat. The daring of poker players is something I admire. A dear friend is one; to me it is like a golden wing extends from such a person. I have dug a hole that is quite deep by myself, deep enough to stand in. I can tell you, it is extremely hard work, the hardest there is. I was a dishwasher in a restaurant once, and that was about as hard as work can be—I say that, but I have never been a miner or a factory worker. I suppose those must be worse. The impression of being materially damaged by the work one is doing—it is amazing to me that it is an impression one can get used to, a feeling that becomes invisible. When I see people using jackhammers without hearing protection, it turns my stomach. I am gentle now, years ago I was not; once, I took a train trip with the sole purpose of punching someone out. In the years 1986–1987, I cut down a tree. I did it with a very dull hatchet. The tree was much like the trees around it, just a tree in the woods surrounded by other trees. At some point, years later, I tried to have a garden right where the tree was. I don't know why I thought it would work. There was no sun there. I outlined the garden with little stones and planted things, but nothing grew. It looked rather like a grave. In that same wood, my friend and I came on the camp of a hobo. Across the street from the house where I lived from five to eighteen there was an aviation plant that is now a Superfund site. I sometimes wonder if I was damaged by living so close to it, and drinking water from the aquifer. I am the owner of a grave plot. My aunt and father and brother died in quick succession and so my mother took steps. She expected I would probably drop off too. When she bought it, she told me she knows what she will put on the gravestone. I hate the inside of churches, and the faces of churchmen. I dislike the profusion of religious iconography. I find it sad that the marvelous talents of Renaissance painters were applied to such feeble and repetitive demonstrations. Any child will tell you the most interesting things are at the corners of the paintings. I dislike flat land. I love hills. I like to be by the sea. Rivers are all right. Streams are great. Lakes and ponds are okay, but I prefer streams and bays and harbors and swamps. Gullies and sumps I adore. Reservoirs are often bracing. I like to come upon an uncovered well. There were two on the land of the house where I grew up. One of them was where I planned to put a body, if I had to. For a long time, I thought it was important to wear a belt. I am no longer sure why. When I played hand-ball, I would carry a glove with me. When I put the glove on, I would become a different person. It showed me that a mask doesn't have to cover the face to be a mask. In fact, this glove was a mask. Once, I stole the girlfriend of a friend. She sent me letters and presents when it was all over and done. She was a great smiler. You could see that she was smiling from hundreds of feet away. I think she was Filipina. She wanted to sit with him and read poetry out loud, and that was enough to make me seek her out, regardless of him. Soon after it was the summer, which is always coming like a veil of blankness to reset the world. More about me being a bath taker: I have been satisfied by two baths. One was in Scotland in Hawthornden Castle. The other was in Japan. All the other baths were not big enough. Even when they are big enough, they make themselves small with little exit holes for the water. I like to read in a bath. I have often read whole books while bathing. They are, of course, short books, Sweet Days of Discipline, by Jaeggy, for instance, to name a recent one. I drink a lot of water and like it. My favorite nut is the Spanish peanut. It is a husked peanut with a round character. I think it is one of the cheaper and less-valued nuts. Often you cannot even buy it because the nut is used in industrial production. Once, some years ago I was mean to my mother and she cried. I never wear watches. I believe I stopped about twenty years ago. I leave my phone behind whenever I can. I hate it. I used to spend hours on the phone with my friend Damon in my childhood home. We wouldn't necessarily talk. We'd just sit there with the phone at the ear, reading, et cetera. Sometimes we would walk each other home. That is—if he was coming to see me, I would go halfway to meet him and we would walk back together, and when it came time for him to go home, we would walk halfway to his house together, and then part ways. I think this is the right way to do it, though people often don't behave this way. In the last years, I have had more verbal arguments with a botanist than with anyone else. We always apologize afterward and everything is fine. I am pretty unperturbable, but he knows what to say to send the flames scorching out of my eyes. Bicycling together, he and I are very agile and have been in some bad situations. He got me onto the habit of generally bicycling with no hands. It is perfectly safe. I have seen him carry a barbecue grill while bicycling. He likes to make things look easy. I enjoy riding a bicycle for transportation and I thought as a boy that if I wanted to do so, I would need to reckon with flat tires. However, in the ensuing time, the excellence of the new tires means one can go for years without a flat. This has been a continual source of happiness to me. I like vultures more than most people do. When I see them, and when I see ravens, I will take off my hat. The work I do is not popular because it is absurd and because only gross generalizations of the absurd, like Dalí's, are popular. The absurd itself is seldom admired, and that is because it is the bedfellow not of death but of annihilation. The success that I have had I understand to be a kind of error, an accident, one that will pass. Therefore, I am grooming myself for a less-splendid future. In ten years' time, I will be parceling out the Spanish peanuts for myself, one per day. My father was an anarchist, and he practiced his anarchism by disregarding all rank, and doing what he could for everyone. This approach did not make him a rich man. My anarchism is the same. The world will not be overturned and sweet communes will not bloom from the fields. But within these insane precincts, we can do our best to ignore hierarchy and to effect exchanges that entangle lives with the debts of life rather than partition them with the use of money. He admired Kropotkin. I find much to admire in many of the anarchists. I also find many of them to have been rather foolish. My eyes are small and my skin is covered with freckles, most especially in the summer. I have scars on my forehead, eyebrow, right hand, right wrist, right forearm, left hand, chest, left knee, and right knee. I had my nose broken by a doctor this year in order to be able breathe through it. The next day my partner had to come and teach my class for me because I was still a bit confused. The subject of the class was Unlearning. I often check my pockets when I stand up. I hardly ever lose anything, probably because of this habit. I like to give presents to people. I especially like gathering dead flowers and plants and making them into small bouquets using other vines as string. I don't do this often. My whole life my family has had a habit of giving funerals to little animals that we find. I am aware that this has more to do with us than with the animals, but it is a real pleasure. When my aunt died, the rain was so heavy that people wouldn't go out to the grave. It was so heavy that the grave was filling with water as we tried to put the urn that held her down into it. It was a disaster. The priest said that we had to put the vessel on dry ground. He held an umbrella over the hole. The gravedigger was on his hands and knees bailing. I was beside him. We were using cut-open Coca-Cola bottles to get the water out, but the water seemed to be coming in even from the sides of the grave. I took a shovel and pushed the dirt in from the side to make a muddy slough and the priest thought it was good enough. That was how we buried her. She was a brilliant woman and used to call me when I was a child and speak to me for hours. She had Munchausen syndrome. The hour of the night when I have had the happiest life is between three and four. I have had many happy lives then. It has been common in my adulthood for me to stay up for twenty-four hours. From eighteen to thirty, I probably did it at least once a week. The thing of which I make the greatest habit is to investigate my habits and break them, reestablish them, break them, et cetera. I do not agree with *The New York Times* that willpower is finite and there is really nothing you can do but succumb to the capitalist spirit of the age. I have been involved with women from many countries and continents, but never anyone from Finland or India. I have sometimes found when meeting a person's parents that the person I am really interested in is not the girl I am seeing, but some shadow amalgam of her parents. Sometimes one or both of them are far more interesting and alluring. It is sad that the exigencies of human decay largely prohibit intergenerational pairing. Unusual people must look at each other across gulfs of time. My mother was in a convent to be a nun. My father was in a seminary to be a priest. Both left and raised me as an atheist. My friends know that I am an almost comical contrarian. The first thing I do when anyone says anything is think: Let me reframe that as the opposite, and can that opposite be true? I think that this is a real strength, but I know it is also an arrogant defect. I do not like to be entertained. This means that I am not interested in nearly all literature, writing, music, film, art, et cetera. The remainder is what I deeply love. Another defect in my character is my love of games. Not playfulness and trickery. I am very playful, and full of tricks and deviousness, but I think that is all right. On the other hand, my obsession with winning games is hurtful and ignorant. I like to light candles, but usually just one. I don't fill rooms with candles. I just light one and sit by it. I love the country, nature, the outdoors, et cetera, but I think what my heart loves most are industrial landscapes in states of abandonment. I also like plain neighborhoods where people do not have the means to hide their actual life and needs. To walk through these places is to be involved in them, to feel the lives. Walking in places of perfect repair and financial resource—what could be more boring, uglier, stupid? Like everyone, I love walking on train tracks. I like going in tunnels and under bridges, across bridges. I like covered bridges, though there are not many. I like when stores are haphazard sharers—half jewelry store, half falafel restaurant, for instance. I like to watch film in order to see architectures: architectures of buildings, architectures of human relations, architectures that are hidden to me now by distance, architectures that are hidden from me by the passage of time. I love to look at a book I have. It shows images of Kowloon Walled City. I have never seen this in person, but when I was in Hong Kong, I stayed in Chungking Mansions. The sheer unfolding miscellany of the physical space—! I like to do Zen training. I am not a part of any group, although I have a friend with whom I share my perspective. What it means is just: I sit in one place and don't think, or I walk from place to place and I don't think. The surprising freedom this affords is something I thought I would never have. When I was a young man, I knew what I wanted to do. What it was was this: I wanted to publish a book of poems and be instantly acclaimed. I did not realize that the world we live in is not the world we have heard about, the world people lived in before. When I published a book of poems, the result was perhaps obvious: no one cared at all! Then you are standing in the street, and you can do what you usually do, or you can do something else, it doesn't really matter. At one point in my life I did a lot of physical training and martial arts and I was very strong and even large. Now I do nothing but walk and I am rather weak. Although as a child I did brush my teeth, it didn't seem to matter. I had many cavities, many many. I brush my teeth several times a day now, floss, use a water pick. I have a gold tooth! I think that this is exciting, and I imagine some lowlife plundering it from my corpse. This is a pleasing thought. There would be little else of worth. I had a band once, with a friend, and we wrote many songs. I believe some of them are quite good, although any of my involvement in the thing compromises its musical integrity. The man I was in the band with is a marvelous musician. When I am having a flute lesson, my teacher sometimes plays in order to show me things, but I am such an unreasonable student that every time he does this I forget what I am supposed to be listening for, and I just listen. His playing is so fine that I can only listen to it, but can't learn from it. I am so greedy about eating delicious oranges that I gave myself a brutal stomachache once, while walking the eighty-eight temples of Shikoku. My partner was equally greedy, although she usually is not, and we ate orange after orange after orange. They were given to us by bystanders who admire pilgrims. We were forced to stumble many miles through the hills, holding our bellies and complaining to each other. I admire people who make their own clothes, especially when the result is idiosyncratic. I once designed a suit for myself, but was incapable of making it. My mother, who is a seamstress, sewed it by hand, and I wore it for years. But I get no credit for that. On the other hand, in Liverpool once, I met a girl who makes one-piece bodysuits and wears them all the time. She wore several in the days when I stayed with her and her boyfriend, who was the friend of a friend of mine. He was extremely charismatic and actually knew every single person in town. You would walk somewhere and people would call to him. The girl would sell her bodysuits to other people who then would do as she did and wear them in the world. Grappling is interesting, because in training it is expedient to learn to give up a lot in order not to be injured. Grapplers are constantly submitting to each other gratefully. I also don't like to go buying clothes or other things with people. I prefer to be in museums alone. I like to go into musical instrument stores. In my opinion, musical instruments are probably the most beautiful things mankind has ever created. They are the most profound instruments of peace. A shop in Chicago, now shuttered, had two floors of the most fabulous instruments gathered from across the globe, and the man that worked there had an encyclopedic, if somewhat vituperative bent. There was nothing better than to go there and wander the aisles. He knew so much that anything you asked would not close a subject, but rather give the impression of a network of hallways, unending hallways pertaining to your query.

His answer was just a gesture toward them. I was heartbroken when it closed. I enjoy meeting people with names like April or Tuesday or Red. I feel like they have gotten away with something. When I am at dinner with people I don't know, I try to get them talking. I want to say the least I can about myself. Often I can learn really interesting things from anyone at all. This is less true of powerful men, who have a series of intermeshed routines that they will unfold for you. Suffice it to say, there is not much to learn from that. One imagines there are things to learn from those people too, but they are harder to get to. I loved wolves when I was ten. People gave me wolf things of every kind, wolf mugs, wolf shirts, wolf posters. My real love, though, was always foxes. I recognize, however, that a wolf will eat a fox, although I do not think it often happens. When I was in public as a child, I was always looking for the safest place to be. I would do intricate calculations about possible impending cruelties in order to find my seat. These precautions were otiose. I remember the names of the children who hated me the most. I can see their faces in a line, right now, as I sit here. It occurs to me that they have probably forgotten me completely. At one time, I owned some guns, with the feeling that I did not want to be helpless in the event that I was hunted down by the government, or in the event of some revolution. I got rid of them because I am helpless in the event that I am hunted down by the government or in the event of some revolution. That helplessness is just my state. I was horrified at some point when I learned that a large percentage of the people who believe what I think are the right things to believe do not hold those beliefs through any process, but rather believe them because they have lived their lives near others who do the same. The animals are all just running in the same direction, and some have their reasons. In a final analysis, I guess you could say that since there is no meaning in life, there is not much to differentiate the animals that have reasons from those that don't, and if you investigate the reasons, it might anyway turn out to be a fractal structure, with more running aimlessly to be found at every self-similar level. I am a list-maker by vocation. List-making is a great deal of what I do. I make lists at night, I make lists during the day, I make lists in my head. I love to make lists. Sometimes in my reading, I come upon lists that other people, now dead, have made in the past, and become deeply excited. I have never known a cruel person to become gentle and kind, though I have seen the opposite thing take place. When I meet someone new, I often flinch pre-emptively inside my face when they begin to declare an opinion. On the other hand, in a different state of mind, I am just deliriously happy to hear anything anyone has to say, and it feels to me completely inevitable, although not distressing in its inevitability. There is no being patient with anyone. In fact, proximity doesn't necessarily indicate a relationship of any kind. One is just sitting there, someone is talking, the world is continuing. I have staged my funeral thousands of times in my head. It is a pleasure that at times in my life I have portioned out. No, Jesse, you haven't done well enough today, no funeral for you . . . perhaps tomorrow. There have been all kinds, of course, but generally they are not the grief-stricken, oh, if only I had known him better, treated him better, et cetera, funerals. In fact, I can't enjoy the idea at all unless I feel it is truly possible. Any fantastical deviation sinks it. This is true for me also in imagining sexual interactions. It has no physical weight unless it could really be in the world I know. For this reason, pornography has always seemed pointless to me. I don't like to be touched by sunlight, so I wear pants and my shirt will often have the collar turned up. When I can find shirts with long sleeves, I will wear those, but I have had difficulty finding appropriate long-sleeved shirts in recent years. When I was in high school, I used to think constantly about whether I should unplug my brother from life support. I wrote out my reasons for and against again and again. I destroyed those notes. I made others. I lay awake. One night, I decided I had to do it. I got up and left the house without my parents hearing. I walked mile after mile in the dark. I got about halfway to the hospital and I sat down on the side of the road and cried into my arms uselessly. I was too afraid to do it. I wasn't sure enough what life was to take it away. When I see someone drawing something, I always look to see what it is. I don't like to be in record shops very much, although at times I owned record players and records, and I think it is a good way to listen to music. That said, I have been in a few really tremendous record shops, including one in Portland that also has an art museum inside it, and one in Japan that is also a vegetarian restaurant. I love to smoke cigarettes and to smoke pipes, cigars, sploofs, joints, you name it. I used to enjoy getting high more than I do now. I now prefer sitting with my eyes closed to doing most things. The American ideal I hate most is the concept of freedom. Ancestors of mine came to this continent in the seventeenth century and founded the city of Newark. Somehow I felt as a boy that this meant I shouldn't need to be a citizen of the United States. In effect, I predated it. This argument was never helpful to me in my subsequent life. I dislike mysticism, superstition, the arcane. I used to love it, as a sign of the human spirit, of the reckoning of the human with the beyond. I now feel that the world is sufficiently marvelous that we do not need implausible self-protected systems to understand it. We can simply suggest possible solutions and continually check to see if they are true. Any fact or idea that has to be hidden to retain its power, well . . . Arcane things, Theosophy, Catholic doctrine, sutras of the Pure Land, secret kung-fu moves, the thing they map is not the world, but human fear itself, human weakness. That's why we are so vulnerable to them. When I ate chicken, and when I lived in Pau, a person couldn't get much to eat on a Sunday, but there was a Japanese man who sold rotisserie chickens and potatoes, and every Sunday we would get one. They were so popular that you had to have a standing order. I liked him and I think he liked me. He knew that I had done some judo, he himself was a judoka and also a kendo player, and he allowed me to get chickens from him without any trouble. The deliciousness of these poor birds was incomparable, and the frites that would fry in the drippings from the birds, oh! The next day I would make broth from the bones and pea soup from the broth. So Sundays and Mondays, at least those two days were solved. I used to live in New York City and when I did people would often think I was Russian. I am not Russian. I am mostly Irish and Sicilian. But I would hang around chess places and parks and maybe my shabbiness was a Russian sort of shabbiness. Various jobs I have held: counselor, tutor, blackjack dealer, projectionist, security guard, pizza maker, pizza delivery person, waiter, essay writer, test prep, dishwasher, choose-your-own-adventure scenario maker, house-framer, potter's dogsbody, Poet's House page, chess hustler, advice-for-sale seller, editorial assistant, publicity writer, typist, leaflet spreader, barista, lawn mower, snow-shoveler, yacht cleaner, air conditioner installer, and of course, novelist, artist, poet, speaker. I was fired from a number of these jobs. Others I quit. The most notable and perhaps useless thing I did in any of these positions was as a tutor when I would visit the homes of delinquent or incapacitated high school students. I was to teach them English. I went to the address given for one student and it was a hospital. I found the student in the pediatric ward. She was in a coma. It must have been some kind of clerical error between the school and the agency that employed me. In any case, I was to teach her *Leaves of Grass* (1855) by Walt Whitman. I sat in the room and read the entirety of it out loud. Various names I have been called in my life: Jess, Jesse, Jesse Ball, Ball, J.Ball. I have never used my middle name, except on forms. The only people who call me Jess are friends from 1993 or before. When I was in high school and reached my full growth, I ate like a beast. I would eat an entire pizza by myself. I estimate I must have consumed three or four thousand calories a day. I was always on some sports team and then when not doing that, I would be playing handball, or out walking or bicycling. I was frantic. Later in my adulthood, I realized that I actually don't need very much food at all to survive. The amount I eat now is so much less than what I ate at nineteen—it is hard to believe we are the same creature, the same scrambling corpse. There is a confusion between myself and the literary world about what should constitute a text. I believe (along with many other writers historically) that a text should be elusive, and that the act of reading a text should make the reader conscious of the life they are living. That is, the text should overflow its borders, demonstrating the complicity of our consciousness with the coloring of our surroundings and the supposed sequentiality of events. To write texts this way, one must stop prior to the point of total explanation. My career has been a very long skirmish about this one point. To me what is ambiguous is closer to the real than what is realistic. To the serious mind, this should be obvious once it is stated. I have had many favorite places in my life. One is in Reykjavík; it is a bathroom in a museum building. There is a window to the street that is usually open. The bathroom is multiple occupancy, but I have never seen another person in it. I have already spoken about the diner in Chicago, and the musical instrument store. Along the train tracks near the house I grew up in, there is a kind of clearing with a lot of abandoned things, refrigerators, cars, et cetera. This is another of my spots. My memory is faulty, but in the late '90s there was a counter at the corner of Twenty-third and perhaps Eighth or Ninth Avenue in Manhattan that sold doughnuts and served coffee or tea in those little paper cups with a plastic holder. The counter wove around like a drunkard, and I loved sitting in different parts. There was no difference between the place and its inhabitants. Sitting there, you were fully a part of it. The handball court in Port Jefferson, the town I grew up in, is overlayed with so many apparitions of joy that it must also be such a place. Sadly, it was bulldozed long ago. There is a map that exists in my head of my childhood town, and as I have gone on to other places and lives, I find that in some sense I superimpose that map atop each new topography I encounter. In a way, then, I am always journeying out of my house, down through the woods, past the cemetery, along the main street to the harbor and the sea, a walk I have taken not thousands but tens of thousands of times. The best revenge I ever took was when I was four. I got all my parents' silver, given to them at their wedding, and my brother and I stuffed it through a hole in the wall. We lived in a rented apartment, a house from which we would be evicted within the year. The space between the walls went down to the story beneath, so we were dropping the silverware between the walls of someone else's apartment. My parents could never get it back. In retrospect, this was one of the more effective actions of my life. I am not even sure what it was that I was getting revenge for. If only someone could tell me . . . When I am reading a book that I don't have the stamina for, but that I am sure I want to finish, I will sometimes tear it to pieces and carry around the chunks, ripping the pages out as I go. I find that it is an energizing way to consume writing. The first book I did this with was *Ulysses* by James Joyce. The most recent was *The Shadow World*. When I do this people scold me incessantly. It doesn't bother me. In any case, it is better that books be read than adored. I used to like to bake a lot, and I baked a whiskey cake that was so alcoholic it made my friend's dog inebriated. The dog kept begging and begging for more, and got more, and the situation just became worse. That was rye whiskey, a rye whiskey nut cake. In college, I baked a tray of brownies that contained marijuana and gave them out in my electronic music class. The professor gradually become more and more frustrated over the three hours. By the end people were sitting on the floor, playing with the equipment, going out into the hall for no reason. That same year, I fell asleep in a six-person seminar, perhaps it was on Falstaff, and the teacher did not wake me up. Everyone just left the room. It was the last class of the day, so when I woke up, the building was dark. The doors were locked. I had to climb out the window to leave. I am a very loud sneezer. On the other hand, people rarely ever hear me fart. I generally do so when alone. When I enter a room I like to find a place to sit down, but I also like to have a clear path to the exit. I look at people in conversation and the first thing I think is, what status are they playing? Are they low-status players, high-status players? Are they choosing their status or has it been forced upon them? Low-status players are always more interesting than high-status players. But the false-low-status play of some is excruciatingly boring. Such a person punctuates their low-status behavior with moments that imply there is more to know. In Mallorca, I was friends with some New Zealanders who had been extreme-sport athletes. They were in their thirties. I was in my early twenties. We went swimming, and the coast of Mallorca has many cliffs and rocky outcrops. They began to jump from them. I was never so terrified in my life, but I had to do it too. Finally, the worst of it came: they climbed a huge rock and dove headfirst from it into the water. It was very high and I stood at the edge absolutely frozen. I had no idea how I would stop my body from rotating in the air before I hit the water. They were there below, paddling around and yelling up to me. Come on, mate! Come on! Finally I dove and I landed in the water like a plank of wood. My whole body was numb and rippling. Years later, I jumped out of a plane, and I found that completely easy. What I thought was, well, at least there's no water to land in. I pay a lot of attention when people speak, but I don't always have very much to say. I tend to remember what my friends tell me about themselves. I like to deduct things, I like to figure out how to make people comfortable by understanding what they are afraid of without their having to say it. Nearly all the time when I lie it is to find a way to put a person at their ease. I do not think the writing of books should be a purely financial matter. I have written books and given them to people, and those people are the only ones who have that book. One of the differences between genre writing and literature is that the genre readers own the texts completely. The characters, the scenes, they are completely theirs. Literary readers seem to agree to a contract that the book will remain the property of someone else, the writer, or some favored group, or worst of all, the critic who best elucidates it. For myself, I use the books I can. The ones I can't I don't keep. If I use it, I get used to it, and it is like a limb, and that's enough. I don't need to understand it, I just need to need it. I have often fled from things. I flee from parties. I flee from classes. I flee from social engagements, from films, from theater, from lunches. I tend not to tell anyone if I am leaving. It seems to me the thing is pretty clear: if I'm not there, I left. I used to hang up the phone this way as well. I would just hang up when it seemed like the conversation was done. I had to stop doing that to some degree because I met with such resentment. The oldest thing I own (from my own life) is a green plastic container that holds my migraine pills. I think I obtained it in 1982 or 1983. I also have a letter from the queen of England, written to me around that time. My dog Goose was once stolen. He is an Airedale, a rather friendly-looking dog. My second wife left him outside a clothing shop and went inside to try on pants. When she came out, he had been removed. Apparently a very large and terrifying man, a vagrant, had approached Goose, won his goodwill, and taken him for a walk. The neighborhood was searched and eventually Goose was found many blocks away in a fenced-in yard. I have been really lost only a few times, and some of those were on purpose. Once, I was living with a friend abroad, and I sent letters to myself with instructions. I wrote out the letters, gave them to him in a pile, had him mix them up and occasionally mail them. When I received one, it said: blindfold yourself. Have someone lead you or drive you somewhere a long distance away and leave you alone to find your way home. It said something to this effect. I have nightmares that I wake from in confusion, and part of the confusion is that I don't know who I am or where I am, but often I think someone is coming. They are not necessarily coming to get me, but their coming is menacing. For that reason, I once wrote in black letters on the wall next to my bed the words *no one is coming*. The result of this was that I would wake up in confusion in the night and read the letters and wonder why they had been written. It was something I could rarely solve, and eventually I would go back to bed. My head is rather large and so hats do not look good on me. In fact, when I go into hat stores, there often aren't any that will fit. I do not think I have a notably large head, and I leave the stores with a great deal of indignation, not just for myself, but for all the people whose heads are far larger than mine. The store clerks are invariably small-headed and flit about through the store putting hats on and taking them off with disgusting abandon. I am always amazed when I hear someone begin again to talk about Sigmund Freud as if his work has substance. I think he is the real intellectual P. T.

Barnum of modernity. I wonder and wonder, when will we be rid of his noxious silliness? The work, of course, has merit—but as literature, not as science. I see someone holding a Sigmund Freud doll in a mall gift store and I think, you are all carrying such dolls on your backs, under your arms, stuffed into your pockets, little voodoo dolls. When will you be free of them? Sometimes I see a film and am astonished by its loveliness, say, *Goodbye, Dragon Inn*, and then it is almost certain that no one else will have liked it, almost certain that the film will be ignored. This means that the moment of my enjoying something is tempered by an immediate concern for the welfare of the person who made the thing. One nice thing about my life is that I am often receiving books in the mail, books I didn't order. A person I know was raised in the USSR and sometimes had books that were hand-copied or typed because there were no printed copies. That he can simply go online and send people books is delightful to him; therefore, when he learns I have not read something important, forthwith he sends it. I sometimes walk to places even though I have no business there. I leave my house and begin walking and then, after a while, I'm somewhere, somewhere I usually go, but I don't want to be there, and so I continue on. My dog loves pastry, and so I sometimes buy him pastry although I myself do not want it. The fact remains, however, that if I am holding a pastry I am likely to eat a little bit of it. Thus my dog is a pastry vector, an unwanted one. When I had a family and was raising my stepdaughter, I was horrified by the Chicago public schools. I had to spend hours and hours unteaching her the things she had been taught. I didn't mind doing this. My policy with her was: there isn't anything that she can't know or be told about, provided that the explanation is clear enough and comprehensive enough. She would ask about all kinds of things and then we would end up talking about them for several days. The reason people think there are things they can't tell their children is: they themselves and their behavior would be compromised by the explanation. Their morality would be shown to be problematic and ill-applied. Although I enjoy watching people fight, I have sometimes been completely horrified when my fighter is beaten unconscious. Then I leave the bar or venue and wander around in the streets aimlessly, sick to my stomach. My first wife and I would go rat-watching at night in Chicago. We would go up and down the alleys where the garbage is kept, and watch the little fellows scurry here and there. Chicago can be seen as a network of streets with shops and the fronts of buildings, or it can be seen as a network of grungy alleys. Both networks stretch the length of the city. Both define it. In my time there, I like to be in the alleys, in the back of things, although the smell in summer is not so pleasant. An advantage of alleys is: the people you meet there are more interesting than those you meet elsewhere. My political views are so outlandish that almost no one agrees with me. Therefore, I prefer not to talk about politics. I have one friend who agrees with me. Because he agrees with me, we also prefer not to talk about politics. Two of my friends and I started an organization called the Poyais Group some years ago. Our business is that we create reveries, unlooked-for and unwanted instances of something fantastical. These things occur somewhere, usually in the streets. The person who sees it cannot believe what they are seeing. And that's it, that's the whole thing, just increase of wonder, joy. I wrote a book about it called *Proceedings of the Poyais Group* and lost it. I think that I will have to write it again, but I am drawing in my breath. It is harder to write a thing the second time. I have lost a book before. In 2001 when I was living in Boston and working at an earth science textbook company, I had two bosses. Each thought the other was the boss of me. So I sat in my cubicle and turned the lamp to blind people if they looked in, and wrote poems, poem after poem after poem. I would get up in the morning, take the train to Back Bay, go into my cubicle, write poems, and leave at five a happy man. Eventually the overboss realized the situation I had going on. She found out about it because I was printing out copies of one of the books of poems I had written. I would print them out and fold them into chapbooks and give them to people. She took one and read it and told me I could keep on doing what I was doing, but I would need to do at least a little work each morning. When I left that employment, unfortunately, the files on my computer were deleted, and I lost a book, *WF JUNE 1978*. It was a book of theoretical art installations and interviews with imaginary artists. That one I proved incapable of reproducing. The overboss was an interesting lady. She was, I believe, a lesbian, rather on the thin side, perhaps in her forties or fifties. She wore simple clothing and had a device for obtaining some harmony during the day's chaos. This was a set of headphones that you could wear, quite comfortable. They played a tone that would gently move back and forth from one ear to the other. She let me try it and I liked it very much but I have never seen nor heard of it since. I have rarely ever killed animals myself, though of course as a meat eater I had others kill them for me for many years. One animal I killed was a bird, which I shot with a pellet gun. I held it in my hand as its little chest pulsed. It was probably a wren. I buried it in the yard and felt awful about the whole thing. I don't believe I intended to shoot it. I was aiming at it and then I had shot it. But that's the problem with intention: how is it displayed but through action? I killed the wren in any case. Two months ago, I killed a possum by driving over it in the early morning on the property where I'm staying. I suppose I was driving too quickly in a place where cars rarely are. His blood was all over the driveway. He himself was very beautiful, as I saw when I carried him to the place where I laid his body, under a tree. His fur was not like I expected. Nor was his weight. I have lifted a koala and found it heavy, like lifting a pit bull. But the possum was very light, was mostly fur. In high school, I was walking by the train tracks and I came upon a body. Perhaps forty or fifty feet down the tracks I found the head, and it had a collar on it. When I called the number, it turned out the dog belonged to someone I knew, a girl in my grade, someone who in fact had been rather cruel to me. She and her mother came to meet me and I showed them the dog. Both were wearing high heels and fancy outfits. It became clear they intended me to carry the dog in a plastic bag back to their car. This I did.

I opened the plastic bag and put the body in. The legs slump together this way and that. It is strange to see. Then I went and got the head. I tried to put it gently into the plastic bag, but I suppose it didn't matter much. Neither of them thanked me. They got in the car and drove away and the girl never mentioned it again. I think she thought that the sort of person I am is the sort of person who does that for the sort of person she is. I suppose she was right. Although I have always looked rather young for my age, I think that recently I have begun to look a good deal older. This is fine with me. At times I will leap in the air for no reason, or do a little dance. I almost always behave immediately differently as soon as I have closed a door. The relief is enormous. When I am in surgery, I get along splendidly with everyone involved, though a friend who is a surgeon tells me that the doctors and nurses laugh good-humoredly at patients and play with their genitalia. When I played rugby in college, I was knocked out completely. My coach didn't do anything about it, just brought me back to the dorms and dropped me off. I was so concussed that

I lost two days of my life entirely. This is not disturbing now, but the sensation in the days and weeks after was astonishing. I have a piece of paper from that day. Apparently in the van ride home I kept asking three questions. The answers were written down so that they wouldn't have to keep speaking to me. The first question was: Where are we? The answer was, Connecticut. I am a good arguer and I usually win if I argue with someone, but I have found in my life that winning an argument is rather meaningless. The real thing is gaining the sympathy of the listeners. I have loaned money to people, sometimes even large sums, and I have not always gotten it back. When I did, I realized that it would have been better not to have. Going forward, I told myself, I will just send money in an anonymous envelope and never fess up. I met my current partner at a prize ceremony and immediately alienated her by explaining that I never read contemporary books. Everyone was very fancy and dressed up and I was not. Neither of us won the prize. As a teenager I bought an impossibly perfect guitar, a PRS. I had to save up for it for several years. When I finally got it I realized that I was not and would never be good enough to play it. Another perfect thing I bought: one of those white Apple laptops. I brought it with me to France and people didn't have them then, so I would be approached and asked if people could touch it. I remember there was a gentle pulse like a nightlight. That year I used that computer to write three novels, a book of poems, a book of prose, and a book of short stories. It was 2005; that summer I met my first wife. Once in the subway in New York, I saw a man standing on the platform. Our train drew up to him. The doors opened. He did not get on. He was wearing a freshly pressed suit and carrying two see-through boutique bags. Each one contained a perfect eggplant. I tend not to disagree with people. I would rather listen. When I was eight, I saw a man struck by lightning in Gring's Mills, New Jersey. We are always in the moment after something has happened. I was in a house in Long Island that was struck by lightning. I once drove in a car in a horrible storm and lightning struck pole after pole after pole on the highway around us. My friend, who is one of the best drivers I know, seemed totally unperturbed. Afterward, he told me he was sure we would die. That same man took me into the gross anatomy laboratory where his work corpse was, and let me dissect it. Another time, he had a spare hand and wrist, when he was doing a hand fellowship. He brought me in and let me cut it up. The inside of the human body—the inside of all bodies! is remarkable. It is not disgusting. What is disgusting is behavior of human beings, the proliferation of military technology, the quest to reverse aging, et cetera. But the shapes of things in the skin that holds you? I could never repay him for this gift, but in the years after when I would speak to people, I would find it is a gift almost no one would want. None of the people I spoke to were at all interested in looking inside a person. One summer in high school, I stood on a beach in the early evening with a friend of mine, Larry, who could do a backflip if he liked. A girl I knew was standing out by the water, and I was fascinated by her, talked about her constantly. It was a barbecue for all the camp counselors.

Larry told me to go and talk to her. I was afraid to. I went out from the group of people toward her as she stood there by the water and I was acutely aware of the deep embarrassment she must feel. I knew that for her to know that everyone could see me trying to talk to her was as horrible a thing as could possibly happen. She turned and saw me and immediately walked back in. I felt so small and worthless that moment, there was not even enough of me to fit in a pocket. On the other hand, people I knew thought of me, even then, as having a special purpose. One year, the phone in the house rang because people down at the beach had injured a seagull and no one would put it down. It was languishing. I hung up the phone and walked several miles to the beach, killed it with a shovel, and then walked back. When I had to give my tenure lecture I read a list of actions that I had taken in the previous five years and explained that since I don't know where my work comes from, the best I can do is give an aggregate of my behavior. In essence, the time writing is no different from the time shitting. I went on to further deface my own image as a professor. I believe it is a real part of the work of teachers to abandon and destroy their own authority. What you say should rest on its own merits. I am very eager to see the ways that people store things. I like to see things that are rolled up be unrolled and then rolled again and put away. I like especially old systems of measure and inventory. In a bazaar, for instance, I once bought some cloth for my girlfriend, who had actually yellow eyes. The cloth was a golden yellow, the right color for her. I sat in the tent of the man who owned the cloth and he had someone bring us tea in little brown cups. He had some way of writing the whole thing down that was remarkable to me, but pore over the image in my head as I like, I cannot remember what it was. I love abacuses, and seeing them used. I went to Japan in 1997, and saw many then, but when I went there recently, there were fewer. Perhaps I was seeing the last of the old generation. They say if you use an abacus enough, you can construct a mental abacus and use that instead, and that therefore you can multiply, add, and subtract with greater speed than an ordinary person. I don't know if this is true. Walking in a swamp in 1992, I stepped in the wrong place. I sank down slowly and then rapidly, and then my progress halted. I was stuck up to my neck with one arm out. The other arm had been trying to push from below, but I was afraid to move it. My friend looked at me. I don't think we said anything. He ran away. A moment later he came back carrying a plank that was by the path we had come on. He put the plank down next to me, stood on it, and hauled me out. When we got back to my house, we both stank to high hell. All the clothes we were wearing had to be thrown out. I don't know where my friend got that resourcefulness, but it later became a theme in his life. He is now a sergeant on a SWAT team. When I cook, I like to use spices. I especially like spices with strange names, but all spices will do. Horseradish, for instance: I don't disrespect it. I like to eat food that is unpalatable to many people. I love to go to Thai restaurants and ask for things terrifyingly hot. On the other hand, I think simplicity is important in cooking, and I like to make the simplest possible dishes most of the time. One of the things I am most jealous of is: old men who can eat an onion as their lunch. I want to be that basic. When I was traveling in India about twenty years ago, I got dysentery from eating a vegetable samosa. The others went on traveling, but a friend stayed with me and visited me in the hospital. He was loyal. At that time in his life, his heart was like a blinding lamp. I do not know him well anymore. The nurse gave me a small jar, perhaps a two-ounce jar, with a narrow mouth. She asked me to put a feces sample in it. I thought this was a re-markable request. When people stop me in the street, I am always ready to speak to them. I am often asked for directions or help. When cars stop, though, beside me as I'm walking, I feel a great hostility. This is because in Long Island people in cars curse at you, demean you, belittle you, throw eggs, et cetera. To walk on the road there is to demonstrate your blatant inferiority. When a car stops, I am sure something bad will happen. The routine in my house is that we do not speak or in-teract until about one p.m. It is important to allow room in life for long thoughts. I like to walk in forests where there is little underbrush, and where the trees appear to sail past one another. In Lourdes, where the Catholic pilgrimage ends, there is a mountain covered with a forest that is in long rows. Walking through this forest is madness, just madness. They must all have been planted at the same time. But why? The town is full of cheap motels, the most in all of France except for Paris. It is full of pharmacies with garbage, holy water, crosses. The squares there are set up like an amusement park with extraordinarily long provision made for crowds and interminable lines. I don't know that I have ever disliked a place so much. When a group of people enters a place laughing at a joke, I feel a little left out, whether I know them or not. I do listen in on phone conversations that people have near me. I do read things over people's shoulders. I will not go into someone else's journal, phone, computer, to find things out. I know how that kind of thing ends. When I have to do something big, I will get sheets of blank newspaper and put them on my drawing board. Then I will sit somewhere and draw all over it. After a while I figure things out.

Sometimes I will start with a list. When I don't know what to write down, I draw things, and in the meandering of the drawing, I think of the next thing. If I am really stuck, I go for a walk and come back. My system involves: drawing board with newsprint; small quarter sheets of paper that I write on while out and about; Rhodia notebooks (graph paper) for planning and lists; LaTex documents on my phone or tablet. The drawing board is used for overall plans for my life's action. The small sheets are used for poems, fragments, drawings, et cetera. The Rhodia notebooks are used for planning classes, dealing with students, publishers, and such. The phone or tablet is for writing out books I have to set down. When I began writing books, I would often cover the room I was in with the pages. I would hang them from clotheslines, or paper the walls. It gave me a real feeling of inevitability and progress. Nowadays, I just go off somewhere and put the thing down. When I am using my phone to do it, I can't even really see what I am writing. I just have to follow the thread slowly and carefully. In wintertime, when it gets to be really cold, I will wear a union suit under my clothes. Once, I had a nightshirt that went almost to the ground. I felt like a character in Edward Gorey. I like to sing and often sing when I walk, but because the songs I sing are usually old folk songs, my partners are bored by them, and find the experience uninteresting. This tradition began because my father was a fine singer and would sing in the car. We had no radio. His father was a real tenor, a serious singer, who sang in the Catholic church in New Jersey. Those wondrous pipes have come down to me in greatly degraded form. I love a tremendous rainfall, especially when one feels the house might be compromised. On the other hand, I dislike going to the beach on a beautiful day unless it is a winter day. I have always wanted to see a tornado, but never have. I have been in hurricanes. I have never been in an earthquake. I have been in a typhoon. I have never seen a waterspout. When I am about to begin a game of go I feel a terror all through my body. My knees are so bad that I can't run for any real distance, although I can sprint very quickly short distances. When I travel, people always ask in surprise, is that all you brought? I rarely bring more than a knapsack, for a trip of any length. Some of my more recent friends are mathematicians. Some of my older friends are pianists. Those are the vocations best represented in my friend population. I have spent hours and hours sitting on the floors of classical practice rooms. What commonality do these vocations share? First, a real curiosity, a deep one, and second, extreme technical mastery. One friend was even going to be a mathematician but became a pianist instead. I can be coaxed into buying an unreasonable amount of cheese. This has happened several times. It doesn't take much. When I am walking, if I come upon a dead animal, I will photograph it if I can. I do this for a friend of mine who likes such pictures. When I used to play speed chess in Washington Square Park, for instance, things would be great if they were great, then I would make money, but sometimes I would get nerved out and my hands would shake terribly. This does not help one to win. The hustlers like to speak to you and about you to bystanders. I usually did not shit-talk, but I always enjoyed hearing them go on. It is a real pleasure to beat someone who has been telling you how badly you play for the last three minutes in monotone. On the other hand, it is painful to have to hand over money to someone who has been explaining patiently to you that you are not their equal. Once, one of my best friends wouldn't speak to me for six months. This was because I did two uncharacteristic things: the first was, I wanted to leave a restaurant without paying; the second was, when our car pulled up at a stoplight, I jumped out and ran away. I think I was not so easy to know at that time. He was a sweet fellow, then and now, so I am sure it was all really my fault. That same year, someone he was intimidated by came to see him. My friend sat there, very nervous, speaking to the man. But when it came time for the man to leave my friend's room, he had apparently forgotten which door was the entrance. With gravitas, he swept open the door to the closet, and without looking where he was going, he stepped in. This relieved my friend greatly. I keep up with people in drinking and always have, but one time it nearly did me in. This was in China, and I tried to keep up with a friend of mine, Loren. I did keep up, but I remember sitting on the ground in the street outside a restaurant and trying to strategize about how I was going to stand up and go back inside to rejoin my friends. The moon was huge in the sky. The air was warm. People were passing, some staring at me. This was in Hangzhou, I think. I did have the idea that I could just stand up and go straight in, but somehow I felt it was not a sure thing. In any case, when I stood up, it turned out to be okay. That thing happened where I couldn't stop smiling. It is the essential obliteration of a human's personality in a fabulous caricature of smiling. When it goes on too long it begins to hurt. I have had the daydream that if things had gone differently I might have been one of the tricky types who escapes a couple times from prison before being hanged. I was astonished once in a flamenco show because I didn't realize that Lorca meant it all. He was just telling the truth about flamenco—and its impossible power. Once I was given a glass of iced coffee in a Thai restaurant, but it was a mistake. It was a glass of soy sauce with condensed milk in it. The waitress couldn't stop laughing at me, which I found charming. Once, I had to follow a man into a bathroom because he was going to beat up a friend of mine. When I got there, my friend was trying to finish peeing and ward off the man at the same time. This was quite a sight. I was told by somebody in a bar that I look like X, a name I don't remember. He showed me a picture that looked a lot like a picture of me. I forget about this sometimes for a year at a time. I go on streaks where I won't look anyone in the eye for a while, and then, next thing you know, I'm right back to normal. I don't like to take the same route there and back. When I lie down, I prefer not to get up again for at least five minutes. I am awed by people who can catnap at will. I have heard this is a trait of sailors, though I don't know why that would be. It was imagined by my teachers that my bad behavior would eventually stop, but it never has. It has continued in all avenues of life, in all grand halls and lowly squats. My grandmother, noticing that I was using the knife to pick up and eat food from my plate, secretly told my mother that I needed to learn to eat properly if I planned to move in better circles. On another occasion, she summoned me from a different state to give me my grandfather's Omega watch, but then reneged at the last minute, probably rightfully. I certainly don't deserve a good watch. The thing that surprises me most about people is how little they care about history, and how they are conversant with nothing that happened before their birth—how they are totally capable of agreeing with any account of such events, having nothing to compare it to. On the other hand, I try desperately to avoid knowing about the news and the world, so perhaps the standard viewpoint is a reasonable one. I prefer Thoreau to Emerson, Whitman to Longfellow, Tsvetaeva to Akhmatova, Rilke to Pasternak, William to Henry, et cetera et cetera. My favorite animal poem is "Jubilate Agno." I went once to the Metropolitan Museum thirty-five times in a row to see two paintings. One was a Manet, one was a Velásquez. Whenever I go to museums, I notice errors: chessboards set up wrong, things mislabeled. Recently in Bangladesh, I noticed that they had strung five or six recurve bows the completely wrong way. I quietly whispered this to the docent, but the news was not welcome. Another time, I was in a museum in France, and I noticed that a painting was poorly explained by its descriptive text. A little boy in girl's clothes was described as being a girl. Perhaps I was sensitive to this because I was constantly confused for a girl when I was a boy. This was for two reasons, perhaps three. The first reason was: My hair was long and lustrous. The second reason was: My name was Jesse, a name that could go either way. The third reason was: I was rather pretty at the time. No one could have guessed how plain I would later become! I like to throw things out of windows, off buildings, into tunnels. I like to throw things. I am an expert rock skipper. I have skipped a rock twenty-eight times. Most people don't realize that such a thing is possible, but that is because they generally skip rocks that are too small. As a boy, I loved to see the arms and armor exhibit. I now question the entire tradition of lionizing warfare. My friend's dog killed another dog one day and nothing happened at all.

Everything just went right on. I have had books come out and people cared, and I have also had books come out and nothing whatsoever was heard about it again. The quality of the book is immaterial. People oversold the business of finding things in the children's literature that I read. Because of that, I really expected to find more things. I had a sense that an enterprising person could just go out and there would be things to find, diamond mines, locked boxes, lost steeds, orbs, talking animals. At the very least, I felt like there should be places to go that other people hadn't already gone. One of my friends was invited, by a girl who adored him, to go with her on a sailboat around the coast of Africa. He declined. I imagine it still haunts him. When the food is ready, I like for everyone to be at the table. Nothing frustrates me more than when I call people to eat, and they decide then and there to begin their dinner preparations, washing their hands, putting things away, et cetera. When I go to airports, I never go through the body scanners. Every time I ask for and receive a pat down. It has gotten to be the case that, although the officers do not like giving the pat down, I enjoy receiving it. I am so used to it. It is like an old friend. In the midst of this comfortless place, here I am being touched, perhaps clinically, perhaps unwillingly, but touched all the same by another human. Sometimes the officers will complain to me about my making them do it. They'll ask my reasons. These conversations always end badly. When I gave my clothing to be washed to a woman in Beijing, a remarkable thing happened. The next day, I left the high-rise where my friend lived, and went for a walk in a kind of shantytown that stood nearby. I wandered the alleys and narrow streets. There were lots of stray dogs, chickens, et cetera. I bought a kind of egg-scallion pancake with a sweet brown sauce and I was very happy. Then I turned a corner, and there were clotheslines hanging back and forth across the street. Rickshaws were coming and going. I recognized my clothes there, all hanging in a row. Of course, I said nothing, but the next day I received the clothes back and they were clean as a whistle. Historically, I have often had altercations with partners prior to engagements with other couples, parties, and such. The pattern would seem to indicate that the stress of pretending to be ourselves is too much for us. A woman that I met in Scotland was a drawing master. She worked in a hospital in Sweden. When premature babies die, they are not so easy to look at. Parents don't really want a photograph of the infant. But somehow the softening effect of the human hand is sufficient to make the image do. She would draw these dead babies with extreme accuracy, just like a camera. Then the parents would receive her work. As if this was not remarkable enough, she would send a Christmas card to those she was fond of, myself included, each year. The image on the Christmas card was her very favorite dead infant drawing of the year previous. I sometimes hide things in places for people to find. I do not make it so that I will be informed. It is enough to suppose it might happen. I left a box like that somewhere secret in Scotland, and years later, received an email to my public address from someone who had found it. In this case, they knew it was me who had done it, for I had been a previous occupant of the castle. There was a store in my hometown when I was a boy that sold kits to make models and also little cars, trains, miniatures. The feeling inside this shop was as though time had completely stopped. In the many years since, I have often thought about whether the experience was likewise for the proprietor, and whether in some sense he was still laboring away in late 1979, dusting the rows of model trains, turning on the shop's lights as dusk came. I picture his house being nearby, and I think of him locking the door of the shop and walking through a town that no longer exists in order to get home. When it is time for me to swim, I start by doing a lap of freestyle. Then I do sidestroke. Sidestroke is my favorite, although I know it is universally maligned. I once tried to swim two lengths of a pool underwater without a breath, and I almost passed out. Stars were exploding in my vision. I have never liked this class of people: lifeguards. They saunter and preen and scornfully glance this way and that. It happened once on a trip to the ocean that I was sucked down by the undertow. It was not a lifeguard but a rather hairy man who pulled me out.

He was very cheerful about the whole thing, and told me I should get back in the water immediately so as not to be afraid. The bad information that I was given as a child loomed in unconnected shadows for the first two and half decades of my life. It seemed, especially in my teens, that not a day would go by without massive data contradicting something I had been officially told. After I swim, I am ravenously hungry, more hungry than at any other time. That is why the very poorly made hamburger and french fries at an Icelandic restaurant near the municipal pool in the center of Reykjavík has been one of my favorite meals. I dislike cultivated flowers. I understand why scientists don't like invasive species, but the distinction seems facetious, just like the distinction between what is artificial and what is natural. It seems impossible for anything to not be natural, isn't that so? The Department of Homeland Security in 2007 chose to capture my wife and stepdaughter, interrogate them, keep them for hours in a filthy room, and then send them back to Iceland. They had to go like prisoners to the plane with an armed guard.

My stepdaughter was eight at the time. When I was a boy, I read dog books constantly, but could never have a dog. Dog books are for the most part books about a boy and a dog. I imagine this is painful if you are a girl. But it is also painful if you are a boy and do not have a dog. I think, however, that the genre is meant for exactly that audience, because the boys I knew who had dogs were not particularly interested in dog books. I have no restraint whatsoever when it comes to the New York City specialty the black-and-white cookie. I will eat one without blinking an eye. What's worse, I might not even share it. As a boy I was consumed by the desire to eat petit fours. I could never get enough of them. Later it was linzer tortes. I know a man in Chicago who will eat a pound of marzipan and show no ill effect. At one point in the woods behind the house we lived in on Myrtle Avenue, I found a railroad spike. I was probably three or four. The object: railroad spike. The object: three-, four-year-old boy. These two things in tension with each other. That was the year I was a carpenter for Halloween. I remember how proud I was. I wonder what my reasons were, what I would have said. When I was first told that a transatlantic telegraph line was laid in the mid-nineteenth century, I thought it was a lie. I was given several opportunities to cheat on my second girlfriend but did not, and I believe she did cheat on me. I hate symphonies, but love solo classical repertoire, especially piano, cello, violin. I enjoy chamber music. For me one of the horrors of modern life is the constant imposition in every public place of bad music. To combat this, I carry earplugs. I can't be allowed to play Tetris or I will think about Tetris for days and days. The pieces just fall in my head. I am an okay table tennis player. Almost all the table tennis I have played is with one person, and he is much better than me. I don't enjoy being in sleeping bags. I was a Boy Scout, but I quit when all the older boys had quit. I was the last one left. I still resent anytime someone wants me to vow. At a symphony in Millennium Park the entire crowd stood for the national anthem. I, my Icelandic wife, her sister and brother-in-law, and our various children stayed seated on the ground. The psychological pressure was tremendous, almost palpable. You could have graphed the hate. It seemed to me then no one should gather in crowds larger than fifty. I like medium-size dogs and large dogs, but I don't generally care for small dogs. There is no selection pressure for them to behave. I am concerned about people who carry snakes or parrots in public, because it seems to represent some inner failing. I have nothing against the snakes or parrots. I hate flags. I hate governments. I hate elected officials. I like crossroads, old elevators, automats, vending machines, waffle makers. I don't want to pass on my genes. I don't think humankind is notably important or special. I believed as a boy that there would be more secret passages. I have not yet found any secret passages. I was told that China would be one thing, but it was another. When I am competing with someone physically I feel simultaneously the desire to destroy them utterly and also the desire to give in to them, to allow them the great pleasure of victory. There is gladness to be found both ways. Wherever I go I make drawings, and I often leave them for people, for waitresses, or in books in bookstores, on trains, wherever. If I do not leave them, I throw them out. My favorite draftsman is Winsor McCay, the creator of Little Nemo, in the beginning of the twentieth century. I don't think anything as good has been done since. My favorite animation is *Hedgehog in the Fog* by Yuri Norstein. I like it so much I show it to my students for no reason. I feel it enlarges whoever sees it. In dreams for a time, I invented a style of movement that allowed me to skip space: to walk, but skip over space as I walked. I managed to keep this ability from dream to dream. But one day it was no longer with me. I don't believe books are about anything. A frog is also not about anything. I like to rearrange my living space every couple months, especially the situation of the bed. When I enter a hotel room, I will move things around to suit myself, sometimes even placing a chair on top of a table. I reject the preexisting order of the room and its inherent preeminence. The house of my mother is full of books. She used to hang herbs from the ceiling to dry. Everywhere you can see early American crafts. Nineteenth-century political cartoons hang on the wall. She left the place where she lived to come and live near me, and when she did, I learned that she could carry this house with her on her back like a turtle. Now it is there, much the same house, but in Chicago. I will eat things in one bite that others take more in order to swallow. I was a hurdler in track and used to be good at jumping over things. I don't like to cheat at games, but I am not incredibly angry when I discover other people have cheated. Sometimes I will lose on purpose, especially if I feel the other person's resolve has been compromised by sequential losses. I like to hide behind trees. I cry easily, sometimes when no one really should cry. I was riding a bicycle in Chicago one night and a van came up from behind and passed, and as it passed, its huge right mirror struck me from behind and knocked me from my bicycle. I was sure I was badly hurt, and the van careened off into the night, but when I stood up I realized that I wasn't hurt at all, not a bit, and what's more, my bicycle was fine. Another time, driving in a blizzard out of Montana, the road became completely obscured. We continued just by gauging the lights on either side of the highway, but they were low, hardly even pinpricks, and my eyes began to hurt from staring so hard. There would be times when the snow would kick up and we could see nothing. I would start counting as we drove onward through the blankness. Once I counted to ten, to twenty. A gust came and there were the lights again: impossibly, we were still on the road. A few years ago, I was walking on Milwaukee Avenue in Chicago and I found a hundred-dollar bill. I gave it to a homeless man, who received it with some hostility. In retrospect, I see I should have changed it for him somewhere. If I see a cat I don't automatically pet it. People's children are not automatically interesting to me, although there have been some of whom I am extremely fond. I can fall in love with people more easily if they are sleeping. I hate it when you are in an argument with someone or they are sulking, and their telephone rings, and when they answer it, they are a completely different person, one full of good cheer. I imagine I probably do this also, but cannot see it. Whenever I go to a new city, one of the first things

I do is find a graveyard and go for a walk. I love the peace of cemeteries, though I shouldn't, since it's based on something I deplore: superstition. I had a friend when I lived in New York who sold books on the street. He was an artist and a chess player. He had been accused of a crime he didn't commit, and although he was found innocent, it derailed his life. But he was one of the greatest people I've met, and what he would do is this: He would make art, really exceptional art, real art, and he would give it to people. I would watch him do it. He would give it to people and sometimes they were people who realized what it was and sometimes they were not. His strength of spirit was such that it didn't matter. He gave me a staff that he had carved which could easily have been in the British Museum. People of all sorts would come up to him while we sat there playing chess and he would know them somehow and talk to them. This was during the time that I was in grad school, and my friendship with him was much more important than anything I did in the supposedly great university overlooking the street where we played chess. The demonstrable force of a person's empathetic insight is rarely visible, but when it is, as it was in my friend, it is a shock. You must change yourself to match it, or you must blunt yourself to ignore it. Once in Garður, I came out of a building with my wife and the sky was full of turning birds. There were thousands of them, thousands in a single flock and turning and turning in the sky. I looked around in absolute prostration—absolutely flattened in my heart and life by the enormity of what I was seeing, and I realized that there were people in the street going back and forth in the face of this spectacle, and to them it meant nothing. They could not even see it.

Acknowledgments

Thanks to: Catherine Lacey, Jim Rutman, the people at Sterling Lord Literistic, and the people at Catapult, especially Kendall Storey and Nicole Caputo. Thanks to Sasha Beilinson and Goose. Thanks also to John Grisham, a man I don't know, on whose Mississippi estate this book was written on a day in December of 2017.

© Lin Woldendorp

JESSE BALL is an absurdist whose prize-winning work has been translated into more than twenty languages. He is on the faculty of the School of the Art Institute of Chicago.